THE BURDEN OF SILENCE

Ramón Barbuzano Morales

No part of this book may be reproduced or redistributed in any form or by any electronic or mechanical means, including information storage and retrieval systems, without permission in writing from the author or the publishers.

The content of this work is the responsibility of the author and do not necessarily reflect the views of the publisher.

Published by Ibukku.
www.Ibukku.com
Graphic design: Índigo Estudio Gráfico
Copyright © 2019 Ramón Barbuzano Morales
Translated by Elizabeth Powell de Barbuzano
Original Title: "El Precio del Silencio"
All rights reserved.
ISBN Paperback: 978-1-64086-376-7
ISBN eBook: 978-1-64086-377-4

CONTENT

ACKNOWLEDGEMENTS	7
MAPS	11
PART ONE **MEMORIES**	13
Chapter 1 My Inheritance Was Waiting	15
Chapter 2 Innocence Lost	27
Chapter 3 The Island in the Dark	37
Chapter 4 The Sin of Being Poor	47
Chapter 5 Barriers to Love	53
Chapter 6 The Spanish Civil War	61
Chapter 7 What Was the War For?	71
Chapter 8 Escape by Sailboat	77
Chapter 9 The Trunk of the Devil	88
Chapter 10 Venezuela, Land of Hope	102
Chapter 11 The Son Leaves Home	113
Chapter 12 Returning Home	123
Chapter 13 Years of Joy, Years of Despair	131

Chapter 14
Shedding of the Lies   141

Chapter 15
Peace and Disappointment   147

**PART TWO
REFLECTIONS**   **159**

Chapter 16
The Truth Will Set You Free   161

Chapter 17
Truth and Pain Go Hand in Hand   172

SPECIAL THANKS   179

The Burden of Silence

Memoirs of Ramón Barbuzano Morales who wanted to break his years of silence

Edited by Enrique Barbuzano González who wanted to fulfill his Dad's last wish

Translated by Elizabeth Powell de Barbuzano, with affection and great poetic license, trying to capture the feelings, not just the words.

Ramón Barbuzano Morales and Agustina Guadalupe González Quintero were my in-laws. At more than 95 years old he decided to write his memoirs about "the good, the bad, and the ugly" of his life. A little before his passing at 98 he turned over all of his notes for his fourth and final book to his son with the promise that his offspring would publish his words after his death. He was afraid of the consequences of telling the truth about his experiences and accordingly lived as a hypocrite all of his life. He became a pussycat among tigers in order to survive. The son agreed to be his voice from the grave and to let the cat roar at last.

ACKNOWLEDGEMENTS

"Rocky, Ramón's best friend"

No amount of thanks is sufficient for the following people who showed great consideration for Ramón and Guadalupe in the absence of their son who lives in The United States. He came often and stayed for months at a time, but couldn't remain permanently. The individuals named below gave freely of their help and company to two elderly folks in their waning years. They afforded them with many moments of pleasure and peace of mind, and the son and the daughter-in-law are forever grateful.

Special thanks to:

JUAN PADRON AMARO and his wife BLANCA RIOS who often checked in to see if they needed anything.

RITA BEATRIZ MACHIN GONZALEZ director of the assisted living facility who treated them with respect and affection beyond her professional obligations.

RAMON GARCIA PEREZ with whom Ramón spent many enjoyable hours arguing and laughing and reminiscing. Sadly he never saw this, his friend's book, due to his own deteriorating health.

PEDRO MARTIN GONZALEZ a friend of the son who accompanied him one day to visit Mr. Barbuzano and from that day forward he went every day to chat with the "old man" as if he were his own father.

FRANCISCO ACOSTA an uncle by marriage who dropped in frequently in spite of the objections of the other relatives who clung to the family feuds of old.

FERNANDO ESPINOSA QUINTERO who by pure chance recorded Guadalupe's voice while she was in the hospital being treated for cancer. He captured this remarkable 95 year old woman in the year 2013 reciting from memory a poem composed for her by her husband in 1936 while he was waiting for the orders that would ship him to the front lines of the fighting in the Spanish Civil War.

THE PERSONNEL OF THE ASSISTED LIVING FACILITY for their care and dedication, towards Ramon who was very lucid, and Guadalupe who didn't want to be a burden to anyone.

THE MYSTERY WOMAN who asked if Enrique were the son and when he said yes, she burst into tears and hugged him saying what an honor it was to have known his parents. He doesn't know who she was or where she is, but what an epitaph she bestowed!

P.S. After the book appeared on the market in Spanish not one of the people mentioned above said a word! They abruptly or eventually disappeared never to be heard from again. This behavior seems to indicate that the islanders solve all their problems with silence and until that time cloak themselves in hypocrisy. We, the editors, are glad that the author did not live to see the last of his friendships wither away.

MAPS

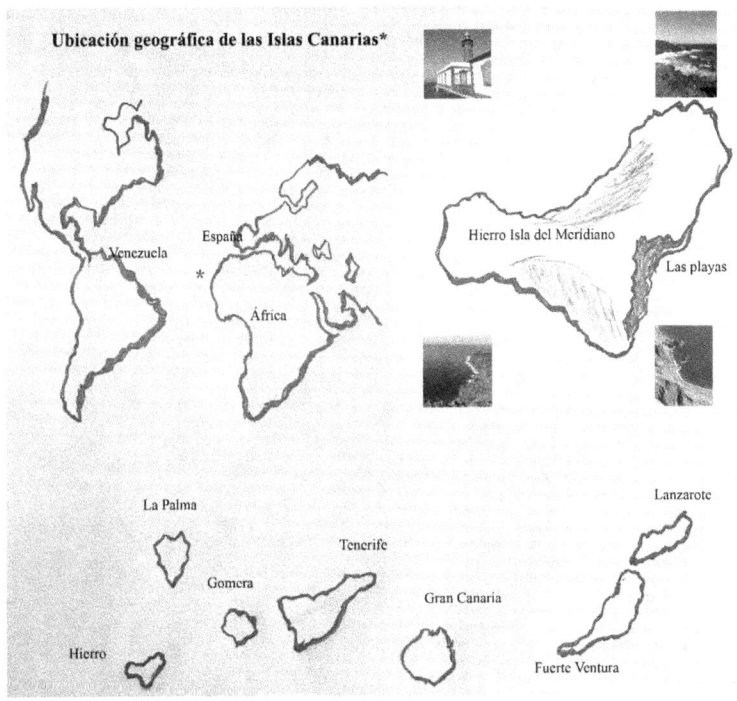

"Location of the island of El Hierro in the Canary Islands"

PART ONE
MEMORIES

"The houses that Ramon built with his own hands"

Chapter 1
My Inheritance Was Waiting

Eleuterio Barbuzano

Marcelino González

My father hated me even before I was born. When I came into this world, his rejection was waiting for me, and I would become the instrument of his revenge. The abuse was frequent and he would never accept the unwanted son, since in his mind I served as a constant reminder of his wife's supposed infidelity.

When he got angry with me, which he did on many occasions, he would call me bastard. In my innocence as a child I did not understand the meaning of the word. I assumed it was a nickname, perhaps a name in honor of being the first born son. Another comment that I would hear frequently spew from his lips was, "You are not and never will be a seed of my loins".

I am writing these pages from the assisted living facility in the town of Frontera on the island of El Hierro, Canary Islands, Spain. I am more than 96 years old. I feel a great fatigue from the long and arduous journey that has been my life. Although the end is near I still have the time to reminisce. My mind is sharp even though my body is wearing out.

The days and the nights seem unending and a profound loneliness permeates my being. I observe my wife lying silently enveloped in her consuming illness awaiting the relief that death will bring her. I do not have any friends that come to visit and my son and his family are in a far away land. Here I feel completely forgotten by my family and in-laws albeit for different reasons, but the result is the same, abandonment.

I am here in the company of others who like me are in the twilight of their lives. Time to think is excessive, more time than life itself. During the long nights when the aches and pains of age prevent me from sleeping, I sit in front of my old friend, an ancient manual typewriter. I write of my sorrows and pleasures and watch the deep black ribbon imprint my thoughts on the pristine white page. It is as if my memories are spilling out like tea leaves to be read, not to predict the future, but to bring to light the past.

Only the repeated clicking of the keyboard resounds in the stillness of the midnight hours when everyone else is asleep. A muffled groan comes from the bedridden silhouette of my wife cushioned by the morphine that calms her constant pain from the cancer within. I stop writing for a moment to memorize her features, and then return to my notes in order to occupy my mind in other things.

Of the several books that I have written this is the most important to me. I am not looking for recognition or fame from its publication. My only objective is to present my story, to share my memories and experiences. I didn't have the courage to tell of the people that I have encountered or of the events that have unfolded before me while alive, but now I hope to empty my heart of the lesions that have been an irritant for so long.

I asked my son to promise to publish this manuscript after my death to avoid any repercussions from those who might disagree with its content. It won't be easy for him run interference on my behalf, but I finally want to tell the truth after decades of denial. I wish to break the silence without the fear of reprisals. My conscience demands that I be honest at last with the people I have known, with my son, and most of all with myself. I desire to truly rest in peace. The opinions of others, whether good or bad, no longer have merit for me.

I fervently hope that this book might reach the young people of today so that they will know of how hard their great-grandparents and grandparents worked. They strove to give their children a better life, and with each following generation the quality of life rose and rose to the present level of designer clothes and mobile phones. The youth of today should be aware of the degree of comfort that they enjoy would never had been reached, if it hadn't been for the sacrifices of the those who left and immigrated to the Americas. Some risked their lives to cross the ocean and most scrimped to save money to send back to their families. Thanks to these efforts the social and economic conditions of the Canary Islands improved tremendously.

It seems impossible, and something that I will never know, but I would like this book to also reach beyond the borders of Spain. There are men and women like me who continue to immigrate with the expectation of finding a decent life for their families. They want to break away from the chains of the indifference of their governments, the abuse of the rich, and perhaps the negligence of family members. Possibly these pages will give them the strength to attempt to do so.

I begin my story with describing the island of El Hierro and what life was like in the old days at the very beginning of the twentieth century. El Hierro was also known as the "Isla de Meridiano", because the original navigational line of zero meridian passed right by the island. It is the smallest of the seven Canary Islands which are located in the Atlantic Ocean off the coast of Africa. It is the furthest west of all of them which made it the last vestige of land that Christopher Columbus saw before sailing into the unknown.

When I was born in 1916, we didn't have electricity, nor running water, and we wouldn't benefit from these luxuries until the1980's. We subsisted by means of agriculture and the raising of certain animals which afforded us milk and meat. Very few products were brought from the outside. Consequently, sugar and rice were among the items that were rationed because of their scarcity. We sometimes did not have the money to buy our assigned ration. We survived by not depending on any product that was not native to our island. We poor Herreños shared willingly with each other because of mutual necessity.

The "roads" were made of dirt and there were no vehicles, except for an ancient truck that brought the cargo from the port, and a rusty old bus that distributed the mail from town to town. In times of bad weather the truck and the bus didn't appear, because the boat had been unable to dock in the rough seas. Passengers and cargo had to be transported to the cement pier by rowboat which was at the least time consuming and at the worst impossible.

On mail delivery day the people would gather in town to wait for the bus even into the late hours of the night with their kerosene lanterns. They wanted to be there for the "canto de las cartas". The mailman would "sing out" the names of the recipients in a loud voice. Many of the letters were then read aloud since most of the correspondence came from those who had immigrated. Perhaps there was news of a loved one in another's letter. The reading of these epistles was quite a social event. Even if the mail were late or didn't arrive at all, the locals enjoyed a bit of rest and gossip after a long day of working in the fields.

Cooking was done on an open fire and we lived in houses with roofs of straw and floors of dried cow manure. To take care of the basic necessities we had to go outside to the outhouse. This structure was a septic tank dug at a distance from the living quarters. It consisted of a simple hole in the ground surrounded by walls of stones which were in abundance in the volcanic landscape. It didn't have a door or a roof and it was extremely uncomfortable to use. Since there was no mortar between the stones, it was especially tortuous in the cold and windy winter months. Even though the island is located in a tropical zone, my native village is at an altitude of over four thousand feet.

Without indoor plumbing in order to take a bath we had to use any kind of bucket and pour the water over our heads and then twist and turn to catch the precious liquid as it slipped quickly to our feet. Personal hygiene suffered in the winter because the water would be cold and, of course, the ritual did not occur in the protection of the house. In this land of poverty soap and toothpaste were unknown. There wasn't any toilet paper so we had to invent and utilize what was available, which were stones (ouch!) and leaves (watch out for thistles!)

The people of the towns would look for a place to sit that would protect them from the elements especially in my town of San Andrés high in the mountains. It was and is often enveloped by the clouds coming through the mountain passes. Every village had a little place called "una gorona" which was a semi-circle surrounded by walls made by stacking rocks upon one another. The inhabitants would get together to talk about crops or livestock, about adventures, and certainly the stories were full of exaggerations and lies. These sites were humorously referred to as "mentideros", the place where lies are born.

This custom of meeting to gossip and get updates was popular before and after the Civil War, but the most important social tradition continued to be the arrival of the mail. It was through these letters sent home by the immigrants that stories about distant lands sprung up. They told tales of men who got rich in a short period of time. The rumors that came by mail at night would by the following morning have gushed throughout the entire island like waters from a broken dam.

The dream of getting rich and escaping poverty motivated many to leave their native country. Those who returned were called "indianos" because they had been to the West Indies in America. They came like a tidal wave overwhelming their countrymen with talk of their successes. They wore leather jackets, chains of gold, suits and ties, and expensive watches. They basked in the glory of the admiration and envy of past friends and preening relatives who tried to hide from sight the patches on their tattered clothes.

The "indianos" would buy drinks for everybody in the local bar and as the center of attention would brag about how much they had and of the important people that they knew. The young men especially would fill with hope like an inflated balloon and would surely think, "If only I could immigrate like them, I could get rich in America too." Sadly the listeners didn't know that the vast majority of the braggarts were great pretenders. They probably had spent every cent that they had earned to buy the costly articles to impress. They thrived by presenting the outward appearance of success, while concealing the reality of failure.

However, the fever to immigrate had already taken hold, and the itch was unbearable. "If they got rich, why can't I?"

Poverty was such a driving force that they didn't consider the risk of losing their lives trying to get there. More than one did succumb. I remember as a small child to have heard of some men who went to Cuba and Argentina. I never thought that one day I would be one of these who put his life on the line to reach out to attain these same distant dreams.

At my very young age these aims were still very far away. My immediate existence was full of misery and in all aspects deplorable. With each passing day my father added to my suffering. It became more and more difficult to weather his stormy outbursts and tempestuous verbal abuses. Being a little kid I could only clothe myself in silence and bow my head in obedience. More than once, when I was alone in the countryside hunting for the plants growing wild that would serve as food for the animals, would I collapse unto a rock with my face in my hands. Far from people I could not hold back the tears and sobbing I would ask myself, "What have I done to make them hate me so?!"

The whole family accepted my father's violent actions against me probably thinking better him than me. They never looked upon me as a brother, because my father branded me as an alien from the Land of the Bastards. They certainly didn't know the meaning of the word either, only that it indicated that I was not one of them.

Even though Eleuterio considered his wife unfaithful, he didn't leave her. He continued sleeping with her and had five additional children giving them a total of eight. During this period when agriculture was a way of life the more children the parents had the greater the benefit of more free laborers. The boys worked in the fields, took care of the animals, carried the heavy equipment, and helped with the harvest according to their size. The girls worked in the kitchen, cared for the younger siblings, washed and made clothes, mending when the holes appeared.

Guadalupe, the woman who I would ask to be my wife, also came from a big family. She was the oldest of eight. She used to tell me how she had never had a doll to play with. From four years old on she watched over the little ones that kept coming year after year. Whenever they went anywhere Guadalupe would be charged with carrying the most recent brother or sister in her arms. There were no diapers in that time period and the mother did not want her dress to be soiled. It's no wonder that my wife adored dolls as an adult. We had only one child so that he would receive all of our love and seven dolls who would never be hurt by being the least favorite.

No one in the village knew of the problems in our house. To them my father was a deacon in the church. Therefore, they assumed him to be an exemplary husband and father. He played the role of the smiling gentleman full of goodness with a religious aura accompanying him like a shadow down the street and around the town.

The "important" men that my father liked to associate with had a little more than the poor. They weren't really rich, they were just less poor. They owned land and animals which gave them power over the less fortunate. To maintain their status of "superior" they felt the need to constantly put the poor man in his place. They flaunted their position of control and took advantage of the other's pending hunger and showed no compassion, nor generosity.

They insisted on being called "don", a title of respect, and enjoyed disrespecting those beneath them. The poor had to work for them out of necessity, but were never paid with money. They received a few plates of food which always fell short of enough for their families too. Occasionally they were promised nebulous favors in the future.

The majority of the time they "paid" the workers with what their animals didn't want to eat and left untouched. And the poor animals of the poor were also poor. The "dones" were sure that these twentieth century serfs would accept the crumbs that they dropped in their path, because a little was better than nothing to assuage the hunger. The rich did not worry about the empty stomachs of others, as long as theirs were satisfied, and their pockets jangled with coins.

These were the deplorable circumstances that I saw as a child, and that I experienced first hand as a man. I got married when I was nineteen and my wife was eighteen. The day of our wedding was the day that we both lost our families forever. My father hated me for being the bastard son and was only too happy to get rid of me. My wife's father despised the two of us for marrying against his will and was determined to punish us perpetually. Alone, but in love, we thought that we were free at last…but destiny dealt us a different hand and the deck of cards that we opened that day seemed to predict our future like a fortune cookie that said, "Don't ask for an easy life, your difficulties will make you strong."

The union between my wife and me united the hostility of both patriarchs and they pushed their remaining children along the same path. The rejection by the relatives from both sides was the inheritance that my son would find waiting for him when he was born. He would begin his life enduring the same scorn that I had suffered.

My in-laws, just like my parents, had eight children who in turn generated a multitude of nieces, nephews, and cousins. These offsprings continued the family tradition of contempt toward their discarded aunt, uncle, and cousin, sometimes demonstrating even greater distain like wine that improves with age. My son would never be lacking in enemies in the guise of family.

From a very early age this new generation of Barbuzanos and González clung fervently to the negative opinions of us that they had been taught. When my son was about fifty years old, he was having a few drinks in a bar in the town of San Andrés. He and several other men were telling jokes and sharing adventures when a stranger silently insinuated himself into the perimeter of the small group.

When the time came to close the bar and my son started to walk home, the unknown man approached him and asked permission to talk to him outside. Enrique had no idea who this person was, or what he wanted, but curiosity got the best of him and he cautiously accepted the invitation.

The stranger began by identifying himself as a cousin; his mother was one of my nieces. He confessed that he joined the group purely out of the wish to see if this cousin was anything like the picture of the devil that his relatives had painted of him. He explained that this was the reason that he had not introduced himself right away.

From that day forward the two of them formed sort of a friendship and they had a drink whenever they ran into each other. When the cousin could no longer resist, he asked his mother to explain to him the cause of such hatred toward his new-found friend and cousin. She was incapable of giving him a reason to justify the feelings she blindly expressed towards a man with whom she had never even talked. "That's just what we Barbuzanos do. I have to follow the dictates of the family," she responded.

It's beyond belief that a person could hate another so and not even know why. Sadly, the friendship between the two of them had to be terminated for the same reason; because the family was making his life difficult. They threatened him with, "If you insist on being his friend, then you are not one of us."

On the González side my father-in-law tried by whatever means to destroy our marriage. He was abusive by nature and in his nature there was no sympathy for others. He had forbidden our courtship, but we got married in spite of it. It seemed as if vengeance was the fire that powered his engine, "They can't, they can't, they can't do that to me." The message that he indirectly sent to his other children was, "Don't you dare challenge my authority." They obeyed and followed his example of mistreatment towards us.

The majority of the townsfolk benefitted from a neutral relationship with my father, the deacon, and with my father-in-law, the landowner. It was much more advantageous for them to side with these two than to associate with us. They didn't go out of their way to harm us, they just ignored us.

Without family and very few friends to give us moral support, it was very arduous to move forward and confront another day of hardships. The love that we felt for each other gave us the impetus to chip away at the mountain of obstacles that were purposely or perhaps unconsciously put before us to block the way.

The "all-powerful ones", as they chose to call themselves, received a certain morbid pleasure out of exhibiting their superiority. They found the means to keep the poor men on their knees making them feel like beggars which they had to be. The only difference between now and then is that the poor man in the old days had less options to escape the oppression.

My father and father-in-law thought that they were one of these influential people and behaved accordingly. We were mere objects to be used and then discarded at their whim. I was the bastard son and invisible brother. My wife was the rebellious daughter and the rejected sister. This was our inheritance, and although it was beyond our control, it became my son's. To some he is still referred to as "the son of the insignificant pauper from the outskirts of town." Those who make this comment are apparently the ones who resent that he didn't stay in his place where he belonged.

Chapter 2
Innocence Lost

The mountain path down to the coast

One day my son as a man told me that a friend of his had commented that we came from the two worst families on the island. I answered him by saying that I couldn't swear to it, but that I was certain that they were not ranked among the good ones. One never knows what goes on in people's private lives away from the public eye.

With ironic sadness a decade later my son came to tell me that this same friend had committed suicide. A week prior he had confessed that he had been wrong about our family. His turned out to be just as bad. He added that he was apprehensive about being dependent on those who treated him so uncaringly in life. Death was his solution before the Alzheimers would place him at the mercy of these relatives.

We humans do not decide when or how to be born, let alone to be able to choose our parents. The history yet to be of our lives begins with a series of events long before our actual births, like a train of dominos that when toppled races on unheeded.

The true genealogy of the Barbuzanos is not very clear due to lack of documents. It is my understanding from the oral history heard in snatches that a Juan Barbuzano arrived to the Canary Islands in the middle of the Nineteenth Century. It is not known where he came from. He subsisted as a farmer and married a Carmen Morales. They had three sons, Eduardo, Andrés, and Nicanor.

Andrés was my paternal grandfather who took as his wife a Isabel Perez. This marriage produced two sons, Eleuterio and Juan. Juan died in 1918 in the fighting in Africa over Spanish possessions on that continent. Eleuterio, who was my father, chose to marry a Maria Morales and from this union came eight children. I was the third to be born and the first boy.

Perhaps as an ominous omen, when I came into the world on June 4, 1916, the night was dark and stormy according to what my mother had repeatedly related. Since my father suspected that I was not his child, my mother and aunt gave me the nickname of Saturnino meaning "figura triste". Such a forlorn little figure who lost his innocence before it all began.

When I was only a few months old, I got gravely ill. They didn't think that I was going to survive. At that time on the island there was no medical assistance. With illnesses it was a matter of luck; you either lived or you died and not many cases in between. One of my aunts suggested that maybe the problem was with the breast milk since my mother was already pregnant again. They took me off my mother's milk and started me on goat's milk. The change apparently saved my life.

This marked the beginning of various events which brought me close to death, but it seemed as if Lady Death just wanted to play and not take me with her. Perhaps the close calls were just to remind me of her, like a whisper in the ear of a lover. I recuperated from the first encounter, but we met again a year and a half later. Due to an apparent oversight on the part of some family members I almost drowned in the well.

They left me alone crawling around the patio that held the opening to the reservoir. These were constructed to catch the rain water since there are no rivers or lakes on the entire island. These "aljibes" or cisterns were quite deep especially in the rainy season.

When I fell in, the clothing that I was wearing inflated and kept me afloat. Was Lady Death observing her little friend dancing as a buoy in the ripples created from his desperate thrashing? Perhaps she laughed when someone soon came and fished me out with a kind of lasso made quickly from the straps of the donkey's saddle bag. I don't know how I survived, but thank God I did. Lady Death, of course, is the afterthought of an adult after many years of musing. As a teenager the idea passed through my mind that many an unwanted dog died by drowning.

Little by little, year by year, I came to realize that the treatment of me was somehow different from what my siblings received. My father roared and my mother cowered; my father abused and my mother hid among her chores, saying nothing. My brothers and sisters kept below the radar so as not to be swept away by the waves of anger. As the outbursts grew in number, the distance also increased. At about five years old the sense of rejection by parents and siblings made me feel like a stranger in our house without knowing why.

It was quite a while before I discovered the reason. I was eleven years old and I accidentally overheard a violent argument between my parents. For the first time I learned how he accused my mother of being unfaithful and that I wasn't his son. She was sobbing so hard that it seemed as if thunder were pounding within her torso, and she stuttered in staccato breaths that it wasn't true...gasp, gasp, gasp. She had been faithful...little Ramón was his son. With cold, calculated calm he declared, "You will never convince me that that bastard is my son." Then he departed to go to church.

That day I found out that the word bastard was not a nickname although I still didn't grasp the deeper meaning. I did, however, see the cause of my family's attitude towards me and the distain expressed by my father. I wasn't his son, I wasn't their brother, and my feelings were confirmed...I was an intruder.

When my father was with people that he considered important, such as the priest or politicians, he projected a very distinct image. Since he was a deacon of the church, he was respected by the folks in town.They saw him and his whole family participating in all of the religious festivals and activities.

He was like the saint who is taken out and paraded around in special clothing, then put back in a corner alcove until next time. He appeared saintly in the light of day, and in truth was a devil in the hidden recesses of his home. His sacred cloak was that of hypocrisy.

My father was despotic and autocratic by nature. He treated his wife and his children without compassion, because that was his character. With me, however, he took pleasure in torturing me in subtle ways, and not so subtle.

An example of his premeditated cruelty took place when I was only six. One afternoon he called me and said that he wanted me to bring him some documents from the town of El Golfo on the coast. He urgently needed them for the following day and I would have to go down and retrieve them. It would be a distance of about seven miles down and another seven back up the cliff.

I remember thinking that I had two options; El Camino del Risco (The Cliff Walk) or "El Camino de San Salvador." The first was riskier with its sheer drops and tight stretches, but it was shorter, straight down more or less. The second route was still mountainous, but less cliffs, less curves, slower decline. This was the preferred way when a family was moving with their household items from the peak to the milder climate on the ocean front, because the chances of donkeys or cargo falling were lessened. The adults would opt to trek down the mountain side at night when it was cooler and with a full moon to light their footing.

On the day that my father sent me down, it was late in the afternoon and it was said that there would be no moon. One of my brothers offered to accompany me, but my father wouldn't allow it. He insisted that it was time for Saturnino to learn to walk in the dark. He knew that I couldn't out race the sun and that darkness would overtake me. In hindsight I am sure that was his intention.

Being so afraid that the night would soon be upon me, I took off running from the house to the quickest trail, "El Camino del Risco". When I arrived to El Golfo, dusk was just beginning and I still had the return trip to undertake. I grabbed the papers from the drawer of the dresser in the bedroom and ran to the other path, El Camino de San Salvador. I knew that it was easier although longer. That was not the biggest problem. My greatest fear was that once I got to the top and before I could reach the village, I would have to pass by "El Bailadero de las Brujas".

I didn't know who I felt more threatened by, the dancing witches or my father. This was an era of belief in superstitions and I had heard many tales about the witches' spells. I was filled with terror, but I had to get the papers to my father. I thought that if I crossed their enchanted meadow before it got too late, they might not have started their devilish celebrations. So I ran just as fast as my little legs could carry me. I didn't know what was worse, the fear or the fatigue.

I ran a lot, then stopped to catch my breath, then I ran again. Soon I could see in the distance their meeting place bathed in the unexpected muted light of the moon. My imagination created shapes among the shadows. A chill ran up and down my body from head to toe and back again. It felt like my beating heart would burst from my chest as if the very witches were calling it to come to them. My feet seemed to leave without me and I raced to catch up. Did I hear voices? Was someone following me? I was so, so tired, but I couldn't delay. It was imperative to get away from there as quickly as possible.

Finally, but not soon enough, I discerned the lanterns of the village not far off. I had arrived! I had survived! I couldn't refrain from sitting down for a moment and that was when I realized that the soles of my feet were bleeding. The children of the poor always went barefoot. I had collided with and tripped over many rocks in the darkness. I had lost a toenail and one of my knees was bloody. In spite of my injuries and aches, what I felt most of all was relief.

When I reached the house about ten o'clock, everyone was eating a fish dinner which is a customary time for the evening repast. My father commented that he would not have believed that I had truly gone down and back up in such a short period of time, if it weren't for the papers that he saw that I held in my hands. They gave me "una pelota de golfo con higos" (toasted wheat flour with pieces of figs rolled up inside) and sent me to bed. No fish dinner for the weary.

Being so tired I fell asleep quickly and slept soundly. It didn't seem like very long before my father came in to wake everybody up for breakfast. He told me to get up and look for the wild plants that served as food for the goats, that I could eat later. I showed him my cuts, scrapes, and bruises from the night before and told him that they hurt a lot. He retorted with, "That's nothing to complain about. If they bleed again, just throw dirt on them and quit being such a cry baby. Oh, by the way, I don't need those papers after all."

From that moment on I began to envelop myself in a barrier of silence to prevent the cold reality of cruelty from seeping in. Complaining only made things worse. There was no way that I could ever do anything right in my father's eyes. In retrospect as an adult perhaps this is why I tried so hard to prove myself to others, that I was a better man than they made me out to be.

At twelve years old Lady Death knocked on the door to say hello again and then moved on. I got seriously ill with what they called "empacho". This is a severe stomach infection common in areas of poverty. It often comes from a contaminated water source and consequently tainted food.

The only possible cures, if you could call them that, were home remedies like teas brewed from the local herbs. If these did not work, then a kind of witch doctor was summoned. They didn't cast spells exactly, but they had their special chants to offer and more mysterious, magical mixtures to apply. In spite of their efforts the most frequent final result was death.

Giving birth in the old days was to risk your life. Pregnant women placed their faith in the hands of what today would be called a "birthing coach". However, in the early Twentieth Century on an isolated island without electricity there was not any training for these women. What they knew about bringing a little creature into the world, they learned from watching the domestic animals do their thing.

It's not the same to help a cow give birth as it is to aid a human being. If things did not go well and there were complications, the consequences for the woman and child were disastrous. Many a mother and infant died in the process. Many a man married several times as his wives wore out.

There was a saying that we heard a lot during this time period, "Hora de parir, hora de morir"; time to give birth, time to die". My mother-in-law bore eight children, but had thirteen pregnancies. This was one of the reasons that my wife and I decided to have just one child. I couldn't bear to lose her and she didn't want to leave me, and the priest admonished us.

This was the atmosphere of hardship that surrounded me as I grew up that other poor children experienced too. Some may have had a better family life than me, may have had a few more material things, and if they were lucky they might have had parents who gave them protection and wrapped their arms around them in affection. A loving home is a haven when times are difficult on the outside.

The feeling that I had as an unwanted child was like two little boys born of poverty looking in the window of a pastry shop and knowing that the family could not afford the luxury. One boy, however, could dream that maybe one day his parents would get him a cookie for his birthday. The other knew that he would never savor the taste of a cookie, not because of lack of money, but because of lack of caring. One was nurtured by expectation; the other malnourished by hopelessness.

All of us, rich or poor, on the island of El Hierro were subjected to the indifference of the politicians. The central government in the peninsula of Spain didn't worry about us in the least. They considered the Canary Islands as just one more colony with second class citizens, In fact the official maps for the longest time depicted only six islands, not seven, excluding the smallest one of El Hierro. So it's not surprising that the local governing body in the Canaries ignored the needs of the Herreños also.

There were two islands that were invisible to those in power, El Hierro and San Borondón. The great difference between them was that El Hierro existed, but San Borondón was an imaginary island of the myths of the ancient legends.

Paved roads, electricity, running water, decent ports, and the first airports wouldn't arrive to the Canary Islands until decades after they were established on the mainland. These civilized improvements were then delayed even more in reaching the "invisible" seventh island.

Of course, these advancements would have been installed eventually. The local politicians could no longer misuse funds when the money came from The European Common Market. They had to meet the needs of their people, knowing that they would have to be accountable for their expenditures.

Today in El Hierro there are public works paid for by the European Community that are of no use to the inhabitants. There are buildings that fell down before their inauguration due to faulty materials. Still others lay abandoned after the funds ran out. These dilapidated structures serve as monuments to the corruption of those who spent millions of euros wildly, not wisely. It seems as if the unwise were not aware of the adage that says, "Parasites can often kill their host and thereby causing their own demise."

In spite of all the above, I love my native island of El Hierro, and it is here that I chose to spend my remaining years. It is here that I want to rest and await my old friend, Lady Death. Things are the way they are, but to recognize them for what they are has its value. Remembering the negative doesn't make the memories so. My sentiments of peace and belonging overcome it all. I have no regrets to have returned to my homeland.

Chapter 3
The Island in the Dark

Mail delivery!

What I am about to relate here may be offensive to some, because they refuse to accept what the past was really like. To offend is not my intention. I am only telling things as I remember them. Everything that I describe in these pages existed, because I experienced them first hand.

For others I may evoke fond or perhaps not so pleasant memories. Feelings that were put aside, asleep in the unconscious, will awaken in their minds and they will say to themselves, "I understand you, Saturnino. I know where you are coming from."

I would like for my words to inspire curiosity in the young, to motivate them to talk to their grandparents and elderly neighbors about the past. I'm sure that they can find information on the internet that will confirm some of the things and the events that I have shared with them here.

When I was born in 1916 life in the island of El Hierro was very difficult and complex with a level of poverty that permeated all aspects of our existence. Many countries that are considered as third world nations have it a lot better than we did in comparison. I remember many moments of pain, but also of pleasure, depending on what it is that comes to mind. Today I can't avoid wondering about how on earth I made it through it all and achieved a certain position of physical and economic comfort that I never conceived possible.

The living conditions before and after the Spanish Civil War were deplorable. It was a primitive system without electricity, nor running water. In order to have light to see, we would use a dried stick from the "tabaiba" plant which grew wild and in great abundance. We tied a rock to its end and then by striking it against something made of iron, it would catch fire from the sparks. From this torch we could then ignite the logs for the fire to cook the meal.

If we were unable to get it lit, we would go to a neighbor's house and ask for a small burning log from their hearth. We ran home as quickly as possible before it went out. If they couldn't spare a log, one would then utilize a piece of dried animal excrement, light it, and hurry home trying not to get burned.

The method that we employed to illuminate the house consisted of taking two or three pieces of "tea" (pronounced "tay-ah") which is the wood from the core of the pine tree. It was ideal for this task because it caught on fire easily and burned slowly. We balanced them across a bed of stones in the center of the one room houses, and kept feeding the embers until it was time to go to bed.

We had to draw upon the same water for all our hygienic needs. First we would wash our face and hands, then the rest of the body, ending with the rinsing of our feet. Since there are no lakes nor rivers on the island, we didn't have the luxury of wasting water. We had to bring slightly salty water from the ponds along the ocean left by the tide and bleached by the sun. To shoulder big empty barrels for about ten miles one way was hard enough, but imagine the additional weight with the water for the journey back. Not everyone had donkeys to help them carry such a load. Due to this hassle bathing was somewhat sporadic, but in the cold months of winter with the winds and fog of the low lying clouds hygiene was put on hold.

Fleas and lice were a major problem in the old days. They were our faithful companions on a daily basis. We would pick these insects off of each other like I once saw the gorillas doing on TV. It was a lot worse for women who had long hair. They would catch them with a comb and kill them with their thumbnails back to back before they could jump to someone else's head.

Most of the houses had floors of dried cow manure and roofs of straw which must have seemed like a paradise to the lice and fleas. In order to control the infestations on the inside we had to empty out the house of all the belongings and spread pine needles all over the floor. Then we would set fire to the needles and let it burn just long enough to kill the invaders, but not too long to avoid the house catching on fire.

This was just a temporary solution, however, because we worked in the fields and in animal pens and walked the roads where the herds passed by. The fleas and the lice just hitched a ride on our pant legs and returned to their favorite habitat. So we lived with the big animals outdoors and the little pests indoors.

Due to the scarcity of water for bathing one could always spot the most popular girl at the dances. Just look for the girl with the dirtiest dress. When dancing the young man would put his hand on the girl's back to guide her and consequently leave his handprint there. Did they brag and show off their dresses with its collage of smudges left by their conquests of the evening? I don't know, but I think that vanity won out and be damn with the dirt.

In the rainy season we could get water from the gullies where it had been trapped in ponds or crevices or trickled slightly from rock to rock. The water from near the ocean was slightly salty, but the water that splashed down the mountain side picked up dirt and debris. So the sea water was for cooking and the gorge water for cleaning.

In the 1920's they began to build reservoirs near or under the houses to capture the rain as it fell from the roof. They also constructed little canals along the ground that would carry the rainwater from the roadside and ravines into the reservoirs. However, every system had its drawback. The ground water picked up everything in its path from the excrement of the livestock to the insects, mice, and lizards that had drowned in the onslaught of the rain cascading down the canyons gathering speed with the decline of the terrain. During several days of heavy storms you might be trapped in your house, because it would be too dangerous to attempt to cross the ravines in order to reach town. Just a couple of feet of strong currents could tumble you along the gorges, and sweep you over the cliffs to the sea.

These waters were often contaminated, of course, and were the cause of various diseases. One of the most common was called "empacho" which is an infection in the intestinal tract. This illness did not allow the body to process the food ingested, and left little balls of undigested food in the stomach which in turn would be painful to eliminate. The local "healers" would treat the malady with massages, herbs, and prayers.

Shoes, which were worn by many in the "economically challenged countries", were not even in the imagination of the Herreños. The first "shoes" were like the moccasins of the North American Indians, constructed from animal skins. Then came rubber sandals formed from the used tires of automobiles. They were named "majos" (the pretty ones), because they were items of luxury. Since there were very few vehicles on the whole island used tires were scarce.

In the realm of the kitchen the utensils were made of wood, and the pots for cooking out of clay. We didn't have tables or chairs so we sat on the floor with a drawer from a dresser as a table top. The cups and the bowls were made of clay and when they broke, they were mended with a wire and a mud paste to lengthen their usage. There were also special trays with a mesh core, but not everyone could afford them. To repair the dishes with this mesh they had to be taken to an expert. He charged one cent for each wire tip that had to be patched.

A little later we graduated to pots of iron and bowls of beaten metals. If these were to wear out, new bottoms were attached by hooking them over the rim. We had to get the most out of everything, or we would have to go without, and that was not always an option if it were a basic necessity.

The houses, if they could be labeled as such by today's standards, measured about 500 square feet with walls made of porous volcanic rock and roofs of straw. The walls were "painted" with a mixture of water and ash from the fires. This ash was also used to wash dishes since we didn't have any kind of soap.

We slept on the floor on "mattresses" made of pine needles. If the family was big, rooms were added by building walls of rocks and covering them with branches from the various plants available. Some were attached or were just a short distance from the main structure.

Any abrasions that we suffered working in the fields or in construction attracted the lice. Taking them off each other was a slow and painful process. We didn't have anything to disinfect the open sores, so infections were common. Since there was a multitude of insects, the battle between man and "beast" was continual and we were outnumbered.

An additional illness due to lack of hygiene was a skin irritation. You would itch all over your body and sometimes the itching was unbearable. Some would scratch so much that they would draw blood. With more open lesions, more infections, and the little "buggers" considered it as more invitations to move in. One remedy was to use a paste of cooking oil and sulfur all over the affected area. Another "ointment" was made from fried beetles which were also very plentiful.

I don't really know how effective these remedies of the witch doctors were, but out of necessity or ignorance, we believed in them. There were all different kinds of these home remedy experts, each with a certain specialty. They claimed to be able to cure everything from an unknown cause of a fever to the curse of the evil eye. Some patients were cured by wishing it so, but others with simpler maladies like broken bones or dislocated joints were truly helped.

The most common childhood illnesses were "empacho" (severe stomach ailment) and the evil eye. Many gave credence to the idea that a person could inflict suffering by just looking at them in a certain way. They would threaten individuals with this special power that they possessed and they were successful. With so many villagers sickly, it was easy to convince people that their magic was the cause.

Many deaths were due to lack of medical attention. Almost half of the infants died at child birth or a few months later. Malnutrition came from lack of sanitation. Conditions in the island improved with the money and information that came from the outside, thanks to the immigrants. Intestinal disorders and superstitious customs gradually disappeared and along with them the role of the witch doctors.

The political and economic situation in El Hierro before the war couldn't have been worse. The power was in the hands of a few called "caciques". Perhaps the "old boys system" is the closest translation. These self appointed bosses were the ones in power or they were in cahoots with those in power. The politicians joined forces with the police and the judges.

Owning land was a symbol of this influence and, consequently, the "caciques" attempted to obtain more land at whatever cost, by whatever means. The land gave them the advantage of food for their families and fodder for their animals, but just as important it bestowed upon them a superior status visible to all. The poor depended on these "rich" men for work that would in turn afford them food for their families and something for their animals if they were lucky to have one or two. They were never paid with money so they would never have the means to buy land and join the ranks of the landowners. What an effective method for keeping the peasant in his place.

The 'caciques" took away land from the unsuspecting by force or by trickery and they paid no consequences, because of their alliance with the police and the judicial system. They were considered the gentlemen of the times and even today there are public plaques in honor of these unethical con men.

The poor man had no defense. When they robbed him of perhaps a piece of land that he inherited, he didn't have the money to go to court. There was no public defender to speak on his behalf. There were several types of plots to wrest possessions away. One method was to move the markers that indicated the boundaries of the tract. If the victim contested the action, the rich man won in court by presenting false documents and arriving with witnesses paid to perjure themselves. The peon always lost the case, because the judgement had been made long before he got to the capital.

In my opinion the most brazen and humiliating way of stealing was by deception. In these cases the "prey" believed in his "benefactor", who usually was a family member or a very good friend whom he trusted. The scam artist, when he sees his friend or nephew in need, pretends to be concerned and to be more than willing to help him out.

The loan seemed to be such a favor since he wasn't even being charged any interest. Also no date was specified as to when the loan had to be repaid. The only thing that the "helping hand" asked for was a signed paper stating that he in fact did owe the money. If the borrower should mention about paying the loan back, the great deceiver would respond, "Don't worry about it. Take your time. Whenever you can." However, the lying bastard never told him about the hidden clause in the document that he had signed, stating that if he didn't pay by a certain date, all the properties would be forfeited because he had signed them over as collateral. It is important to realize that in the old days very few people in this isolated island knew how to read and write very well. So the man often times was ripped off not due to carelessness, but to ignorance.

And so it was that many an innocent man lost his land for a relatively small quantity of money, because the sophisticated thief would not want to invest too much up front in case the quarry escaped the trap. Also if there were little money involved, the loan would seem more plausible and the wish to help more credible.

The instigator got away with the "robbery" because it was legal, although not moral. The worst thing of all was that the fallen prey would not only feel like a fool, but he would have to pass by his beloved properties and see them in the hands of this treacherous friend or relative for the rest of his remaining years.

All of this would be altered with the advent of the returning immigrants. The economic power would no longer be in the hands of the few. The money brought back by the "indianos", those who had been to America, created a new social class. The standard of living improved greatly, but the old customs were resistant to change. Today there are less people abused, but there are more abusers.

We now have electricity and indoor plumbing, plus we have acquired an endless list of the many sought after modern material things that we never dreamed of having. For many the past is distant history, but our future is very uncertain. I believe that the Herreños will have to immigrate once again. The problem facing the immigrant today is to where and to do what?

The countries that had received foreigners with open arms, for example Venezuela, can no longer do so. Now they are the ones immigrating. Technology has eliminated many kinds of jobs, but most of the Canary Islanders do not have the necessary technical training or degrees. It would be a challenge for them to survive and provide for their families in a foreign land.

We have been living in a dream world of comforts that people do not want to wake up from, but sooner or later they will be forced to face the reality of the current situation. The truth is that in our little island of El Hierro we lack natural resources, and we do not produce anything that is marketable. There are no industries to speak of. The agricultural fields are abandoned. We don't have the knowledge nor the initiative to move forward. Some of the younger generation are living off their parents and others are being sustained by the equivalent of a welfare system. Nationwide unemployment is more than 50%.

As if this were not enough to our detriment, we have allowed the politicians to convert the island into an economic parasite, and now we have no other choice but to live in the bleached out environment. The honeymoon is over, and some need to be shoved out of bed. The European Community will not continue to tolerate nor support the unfettered waste of their subsidies. If there were a song dedicated to this fiasco, it would be to the music, "Where have all the flowers gone?", but with the title of "Where has all the money gone?" And the tempo would be tempestuous, like the "Overture of 1812".

In the time of poverty we all worked in whatever we could to obtain the basic needs. We lived from day to day and we had very little. In spite of all this today we can speak of the bad years with good memories. I am afraid that the young people of the Twenty-first Century, when it comes time for them to remember their old days, will have bad memories of the good years.

Chapter 4
The Sin of Being Poor

The two basic necessities of the poor man

When I see how we give so little value to the comforts that we enjoy today, it takes me back to my childhood. In those times I did not really know that I was poor, because most of the people around me were living under the same conditions. Of course by today's standards I now realize the depth of our poverty. I walked without shoes and wore tattered clothes. My pants were short and made of many scraps of cloth with only one strap to hold them up. They were faded from long use and repeated repairs so that the original colors and designs were like an unknown mystery to be unraveled.

The winters were very cold and we didn't have anything like a coat or jacket. In order to protect myself from the elements, I would use a potato sack as a cape, but I still found myself shivering, my teeth rattling like the beans inside a maraca. I would creep along close to the stone wall away from the wind like a little mouse seeking shelter.

The patched "uniform" of poverty was the outfit that I wore on my first day of school. I barely learned to read and write and do basic math. I didn't like school very much, so I was glad when my father took me out to work in the fields. Subsistence was far more important than book learning to the poor farmers.

At twelve years old I began to work on the construction of the public highways from sunrise to sunset. They paid me two "pesetas" for twelve hours and I had to hand them over to my father at the end of day. I never imagined that this kind of labor would be my first job as a man after the Spanish Civil War.

As a little boy, when I would injure my feet due to lack of shoes, I would throw dirt on the wound to stop the bleeding as my father had taught us. One day it occurred to me to make a kind of slipper out of goat hide, but when it rained I had to take them off and carry them. When wet, they would get all squishy and slimy. If I used them when it was hot, I would slip and slide on the dry grass so I had to be extra careful not to fall. I was trying to avoid infections on my feet, because sometimes you had to drain the sores with a knife.

My father made me work longer, harder, and more often that my brothers. Very rarely did I have a free day, but once in a blue moon there would be a Sunday afternoon when I could play with the other children. We spun tops from a little wooden stick which would launch them into a path of dizzying circles, or we shot marbles. I remember the marbles with their pretty colors as special treasures reminiscent of a rare day of freedom. The rest of the time I spent watching over the livestock and tending the crops. My father seemed to take delight in waking me up, while my brothers and sisters slept on. He would send me to round up the few cows and goats to bring them in for milking.

Often in barren times ingenuity sprouts up to help you to survive; in other words "necessity is the mother of invention". In my case I was always very good with my hands. As a child to distract myself from the distain surrounding me, I would attempt to make things. This attitude came to serve me well as an adult to attain a decent living for my family. I learned how to plow, to harvest the crops, to thresh the wheat, to winnow the seeds from the husks, and to reap the grains. The life of the farmer had a certain appeal for me and I wanted to master all that I could. Today I think that part of my motivation was to try to please my parents with the hope that someday they might throw a little appreciation my way, like seeds being sowed in the furrows. However, it was not to be. Eventually I felt happier alone in the countryside than with the family in the house.

As the years went by I continued to observe the "experts' and I discovered how to make many things. All those who had a special skill took steps to keep their work a secret. However, they didn't think that they had too much to fear from a kid and I was more sneaky than they were cautious. I would subtly watch what they did and committed it to memory. I practiced by producing things for me and when ready I would show them to some people. Often they would buy the item, of course paying me with food not currency.

After having successfully made halters and cinches for the donkeys, I decided to try to construct the saddle pack, which consisted of two "fanny" packs on each side to carry the cargo, and padding to avoid chaffing, plus the under belly of cinches, also padded. I started by mulling over in my mind as to how I was going to do it. The saddle maker would never agree to teach me, nor let me observe, so I had to figure it out by myself. I came to the conclusion that if I bought an old one and took it apart, I could study the pieces and practice assembling them until I got it right. So I began to save my money, which would take a while, to buy a used one from a neighbor. When I asked him to set it aside for me until I had the means of buying it, he was perplexed since he knew that I didn't even have a donkey. So I explained to him why I wanted it. He burst out laughing and ended up giving it to me free of charge.

It was a very old saddle bag and I bet that he thought that I would never be able to pull it off. I carried it home anxious to get to work on it. I spent all morning to take it apart. I spread all the pieces out on the ground to study them better. Then I put them together and took them apart, together, apart, until I became confident over the next few days. Sunday was the big day when I would make the new one from scratch. Slowly it began to take shape, the interior, the lining and the sewing of it. I was so excited to see it forming before my very eyes. I had mastered another skill! When I held it up for the neighbor to see, he was so surprised and impressed that he purchased it.

By using the same method of observation I became a barber. There was only one barber on the whole island who traveled from village to village. Whenever anyone that I knew went to the barber I was right there at their side so I could study the art of cutting hair. It would be another talent that I could add to my collection, like the notches on the gun in the old west, not to kill, but to survive. In fact they assigned me the job of barber in the army which got me out of peeling potatoes. After the war I continued to cut hair, but I never asked for money. As a thank you they would give me fruit or vegetables.

This is how my life began as a teen and as a young man. Today I have the great satisfaction of having accomplished many things without help from anyone. I built my houses with my own hands, little by little, year by year, as I had done all of my life with patience and dedication. In constructing the houses I initiated each project with stacking and cementing the rocks for the foundations and would stop only when I ran out of materials. If I didn't have the funds to purchase more, I would labor for others and save the money to acquire more supplies.

I laid the floors, made the doors, the furniture, the window frames, the reservoirs to conserve the water. I prepared the corrals for the animals and the "storage sheds" made of stone.The only thing that I needed assistance with was the placing of the roof. Obviously the items that I created were not perfect because of the privation of formal training, but the more I fabricated them the better the quality.

These accumulated proficiencies that I amassed over the years permitted me the capability of earning a decent living and feeding my family both in the Canary Islands and Venezuela. I rarely threw away an old lock, for example, without first determining if I could invent a new key for the missing one. I saved everything that others considered junk. My daughter-in-law loved the little lampshade that I made for her out of an old milk carton; once painted and decorated you couldn't discern its origin. My wife was also very talented in repairing clothes or making "new" ones out of halves of old dresses. She was an excellent cook too and didn't waste food. Her mystery soups, as my daughter-in-law called them, were delicious, full of a little bit of this and a little bit of that. No leftovers were leftover.

By making things ourselves and not having to pay others led us out of the abyss of poverty where many others remained stuck. We had our houses and with the rent that came to us from several of them, we were able to enjoy quite a comfortable life in our golden years. Our relative "wealth" was modest, but unexpected. We had overcome miserable conditions alone without outside aid thanks to the efforts of our labors. We fought constantly against those who insisted on placing a myriad of barriers in our path. Now we can live without great worries, because we are no longer dependent on anyone. My wife and I, in spite of the numerous tragedies and disappointments, have had many years of happiness because we were together. The unsurpassed love that we felt for each other gave us the strength to conquer all.

Chapter 5
Barriers to Love

Opening to the well

At eighteen years old I fell in love with the woman who would become my wife and she had just turned seventeen. Even though we were so young we married a year later on January 1st, 1936 without the consent of either family. My wife's father would never forgive her for having eloped in the middle of the night after he had expressly forbidden her to have anything to do with me. He not only disapproved, but he felt that it was his right to punish us for such effrontery. My family due to the hatred that my father had always harbored toward me had no objection to my nuptials. I'm sure that he saw it as a way of getting rid of me. The day of the wedding we both lost our families forever, hers for lack of obedience, and mine for lack of caring. The two patriarchs had in common two things: maliciousness and vengeance.

When my father-in-law discovered that Guadalupe and I were still in contact, he attempted to end the courtship. He claimed that I was a miserable poor man without a future and not worthy of marrying a daughter of his. He insisted that she not even talk to me again, to keep her distance, and if she didn't, he would keep her locked up at home. We didn't obey, because we couldn't. Our love was too compelling. We saw each other in hidden recesses accompanied by friends who also carried messages for us. We maintained our relationship, but with each day it got more and more unmanageable to sustain the pretense of indifference. Love has a way of lighting up your face from the warmth from within.

At the dances she was allowed to have only one dance with me so that Marcelino would not come across as despotic in the eyes of the townspeople. When he found out that we were still meeting each other, he became more abusive behind the closed door of his domain. "If you are not going to do as I say the easy way, then we will do it the hard way. You will obey me!"

From then on she was not permitted to attend the dances period. While her brothers and sisters went out on Sundays, she was kept at home to work. Remind you of a well known fairy tale? The dances and the festivals were the only diversions that the young people had. It was a time for boyfriend and girlfriend to meet and talk and to stroll through the plaza for everyone to see that they belonged together. This beautiful custom of courtship was negated to us and our forced separation made life unbearable.

One day I received a message from her via one of her sisters in which she pleaded with me to go away and leave her alone if my love for her was not true. If I, however, truly did love her, then she implored me to take her out of her father's house. The abuses were growing stronger and more frequent. I sent word back that I would arrange everything for our marriage that she just needed to give me a little time to set things in motion.

With notes sent in secret we were finally able to agree on a plan and one night after her parents had gone to bed and with her sister as co-conspirator, they left the house in darkness to join me at the chosen rendezvous point. I had brought with me the mayor, two witnesses, and a married couple who would receive my wife-to-be in their home for the required month of waiting until the bands had been made public. This custom gave anyone who objected to the union of the two people named time to respond, such as a current wife. Marcelino, the father of the pending bride did not object, because he did not want her back. He declared to his remaining offsprings that he did not have eight children, only seven, and that they were not to mention the name Guadalupe in his house ever again.

I had prepared the elopement in this way to protect the dignity and reputation of my future wife. This was very important to her and to me, since we came from a little town where gossip was a favorite pastime. I remember that the night was cold, but there was a full moon peeking down on us between the clouds. We were located on the perimeters of the village and the weight of waiting was becoming a burden of doubt. Did she change her mind? Why were they taking so long? Did the father discover their flight? I shuttered to think of the punishments that would be hers if we were not successful.

Just when all hope had trickled to my toes, I saw them moving toward us. Guadalupe said goodbye and thank you to her sister. I took my fiancee's hand in mine and watched as her sister walked away and disappeared into the darkness. I prayed that she would not get caught sneaking back into the house. When we could no longer distinguish her distant form, I turned to my beloved and wrapped her in my cape as a symbol of the protection that I planned to provide for her the rest of our life together.

I can recall the moment in my mind as if it were yesterday. The clouds cleared and the sky lit up with a thousand stars. A few fleeting stars drew chalky lines across the firmament and the volcano, El Teide, on the nearby island of Tenerife stood out in all its majesty. We both felt as if that night with its spectacular beauty was a sign from God blessing our union. We expressed to each other the thrill of the expectation of being together forever more. Perhaps each of us thought deep within that our families would eventually accept our marriage with time. It doesn't cost anything to dream, but in our case it never came to be. They never accepted us again as part of their family unit. If only they had just ignored us, but the two patriarchs were determined to castigate us in word and in deed.

On January 1st, 1936 we celebrated our wedding. We invited members of both the Barbuzanos and the González and not a one came. The only people present at the meager ceremony were the godparents for the marriage and two of their children as witnesses. We toasted with a bottle of wine which was all that I could afford and I gave all of my savings of seven "duros" (about five dollars) to my godfather to pay the priest. We spent our honeymoon night in their storage shed along with the farm implements and slept on a borrowed bed, and that evening was one of our happiest days.

We rented a little shack and worked hard to get started on building our future. My wife handled well the little bit of money we earned. She spent it only on the bare necessities. Before breaking ties with her family Guadalupe had lived quite a comfortable life for the standards of the time. She never had had to work in the fields, digging, planting, pruning, and now she did. She worked along side me and never complained.

By getting married we isolated ourselves though not by choice. Yet we were happy enjoying each other's company and making plans for the years to come. We fantasized aloud of the possibilities we could attain with hard work, patience, and our labors laced in love. We were finally together and that was all that counted, but we soon found out that our harmony was to be short-lived. Three months after getting married war broke out in Spain and the historic Spanish Civil War had a catastrophic effect on our life. When they began to draft the young men in the Canary Islands, I knew that they would soon be coming for me. The idea of leaving my young wife alone tore me apart. Of course war is difficult on everyone, but my wife had no one for support, as a soldier has his comrades, or the widows have their families.

I received my notice to report to the military headquarters, and they informed me that I was going to be sent to the front lines of battle in northern Spain. They gave me five days to prepare and put my affairs in order. In my desperation I tried to convince myself that the reality of war was not true. I felt guilty as if I were abandoning my wife and the pain of her suffering alone without kinfolk was greater that any fear that I might have sensed for myself as a soldier. The anguish propelled me to decide to humble myself before my father-in-law. I would beg him to take back his daughter and not to leave her cast aside. I didn't dare approach him in person, because I was quite certain that he would refuse to see me. So I wrote him a letter from Tenerife just before being shipped out to Morocco.

To Mr. Marcelino González,

With all due respect I dare to address this letter to you in this the most difficult moment of my life. I am deeply worried about what will happen to my wife with me away at war. I humbly beg of you to forgive your daughter for having married me against your wishes. I implore you not to leave her all alone and destitute since I will not be able to help her in any way. I could very well die in battle and never return. We all make mistakes in life, but she deserves a second chance and your forgiveness. I am pleading on my knees, please please, please, do not abandon her.

From Ramón Barbuzano

In the 1950's Marcelino González died (from the after effects of a kick in the head by a donkey) and among his possessions his family found my letter crumbled in a drawer of an old wooden dresser along with other papers dirty and yellowed with age. They stumbled upon it by accident while they were looking for documents related to their inheritance. None of them were aware of this letter that I had written. Apparently the father had read it, hid it, and did nothing. His offsprings also thought that the letter was of little importance, and told one of the sister to burn it along with the other garbage. She decided not to do so and instead delivered it to my wife. What was her motive, to cause more pain, or to help a sister close the book on a past chapter?

When I left for the war, my wife was pregnant. Expecting a child did not make the situation any easier, but if by chance I should not survive, she perhaps would be consoled a little with the child as a memory of me. He or she would be a product of our love. Due to her condition my parents took her in, but the pregnancy went awry and she lost the little baby girl. When the news of the tragedy reached me at the battle front by the way of a new recruit, I could only imagine the agony that my wife was going through…the abandonment, the hostility, the fear of never seeing her husband again, and then on top of everything else, the loss of the child. I was tortured by the idea that with the death of her baby the one positive ray of sunshine in her life was extinguished too. She had so little to hang her hopes unto. I just had to return to her!

Under these circumstances my father-in-law saw an opportunity he couldn't resist. He would bring his errant daughter home. My parents encouraged her to go with her father since they didn't really want her with them either. Marcelino was not motivated by repentance, nor love for his daughter. He took her in because now he would have a servant without the financial burden of salary, nor additional mouths to feed such as a child. With luck the son-in-law wouldn't come home alive and Guadalupe would be dependent on him again for her survival. She was not embraced as a daughter, nor as a sister; she was only considered as the live-in maid who washed, ironed, made and mended clothes, who cooked the food and washed the dishes, who made the beds and cleaned the floors and swept the patio.

My poor wife had no other alternative but to take each day as it came. She possibly put any hope to sleep deep inside of her as if in hibernation until the day the nightmare of the war would be over. Did she ever contemplate that she also, as her husband, might not survive the war?

My father-in-law had no compassion because he had no conscience and this was the example that he set for his children. When one thinks only of oneself, in spite of the possible repercussions for others, then one always puts his own interest above all else. This philosophy of life dictates behavior and their ensuing treatment of the daughter and sister was inhuman. They succeeded in destroying her spirit and robbing her of her dignity. They converted her into a victim who suffered for the rest of her life. "What did I do wrong for them to hate me so? Don't family have to love you because you are all from the same gene pool? Doesn't the common blood connect you?" She was never able to overcome this inferiority complex. Even when bedridden due to illness she bemoaned, "Why am I so unlovable?"

The mother and the seven siblings set her apart. In their minds she was simply there to serve them. When my son and I asked them many years later why they had shown such contempt toward their eldest sister, many remained silent because they could not defend their actions. A few, like the mother, tried to justify their lack of compassion by blaming the vindictive character of the head of the household. Others negated that they did anything wrong, and still others hid behind the words of "that's a lie". I learned of all of this abuse when I returned from the war. I found my wife with a war of her own without ammunition to fight back and no one on her side to watch her back. Selfishly I guess that I am glad that I didn't know about all of this when I was far away. I probably would have been so angry that I would have been shot for desertion trying to reach the wife who needed me so.

Chapter 6
The Spanish Civil War

The young soldier and his wife

The Spanish Civil War broke out in May of 1936 and in the very same month the forces of General Francisco Franco came to the remote island of El Hierro to round up the young men to ship them off to war, almost like the slave traders of old who raided villages to supply their need for manpower. Without a choice, without an inkling of the premise of war, we were obligated to become soldiers. Either join or be shot. At nineteen, of course, I was afraid of dying, but my fear was even greater thinking of leaving my young wife alone and rejected by both families. The apprehension of the war and of my wife made me crazy with desperation. Circumstances beyond my control were dictating the direction of our life and there was absolutely nothing that I could do.

So I departed with the other recruits from the island of El Hierro and we were sent to the town of Guimar in Tenerife, and then to Olla Fria. Two weeks later the troops were put on an old ship called " El Aragón", destined for the port of the Spanish possession Ceuta in Africa. It was an old and neglected vessel. The cargo holds were covered with dried animal manure of long ago and the smell and the appearance were depressing. Most of us had never left our island and therefore had never been to sea. The seasickness brought on the vomiting where we slept and continued on the deck. There was no escape from the sight and the odor by day or from the sound and the odor by night.

The food that they gave us was sparse and bad. It consisted of dried bread and canned meats. There were no provisions for personal hygiene and we were already sleeping on filthy floors. When I think of the deplorable conditions in which they had us contained, it seems inconceivable then and now. They treated us as animals even though they were asking us to risk our lives on their behalf.

After a couple of weeks in Ceuta they transferred us to another ship that was even worse. We had to climb down into the holds by means of a ladder made of tubes. The aroma was even more pungent that the previous stink. Four days later we arrived to El Zoco del Araba, state of Saque in Africa where we remained a month awaiting orders to move out. Finally we disembarked in Morocco and ten days later into another "floating garbage bin" on route to the peninsula. Our ultimate destination would be the town of Teruel in northern Spain where the fighting was said to be the fiercest.

Before leaving Morocco I had the chance to send a letter to my beloved wife. While biding my time until the next round of orders shifted our location my mind churned like a whirlwind. I was unable to rest with the talk of the recent degrading voyages, of the families far away, of possible death in distant provinces. I felt enveloped in a dark cloud of depression that I could not shake off or seem to come out of. So to distract myself I composed this poem to the one I cherished just in case I might never be able to tell her of my feelings in person once again.

"Poem from the Heart"

I am writing you from Morocco
only to assure you that
because I love you so
all my joy has disappeared.

I live very saddened.
I am always thinking of you.
The happiness of having spent
time at your side has gone away
and is a distant memory.

I want to be able to tell you
with words of great tenderness
that my love for you was the obsession that
gave me the courage to seek you as my wife.

When I sit down to write you
be it at night or during the day,
my heart feels deep anguish
and beats in such a way
that if it were not encased in my chest,
it would burst forward to be free.

I don't want to tell you what my life is like.
Instead I will try to convey my thoughts of you
and put them into words with paper and pen.
I am not going to share my greatest sufferings,
because the times that fear threatens to overtake me,
I sense your love and I feel nothing else.

From the moment, dear heart,
that they took you away from me,
I am not conscious of having one minute of peace.
My only one, you are the focus of my life.
You are my loyal supporter.
When violence creeps into our lives,
I can only say that both of us have to endure.

My jewel, I despair when I reflect on our situation
and smother my inner sobs with the hope of our reunion.
This is my everlasting wish,
this is what I envision,
to cross the Straights of Gibraltar into battle
and yell "Viva Espana!"
in order to extinguish this turmoil
and be free to come home to you.

Note: *The son of Ramón and Guadalupe heard this poem for the first time when a friend visited his mother in the hospital after an operation for cancer which was not successful. She was to die just months later and this poem could have been lost forever, if it hadn't occurred to him to tape the conversation. At the age of 96 and recuperating from surgery this remarkable lady was able to recite from memory the above poem after 77 years.*

We left Morocco for the port of Cádiz in a boat as bad as all the others. We crossed the Straights of Gibraltar with all of the lights turned off so that the enemy would not discover our approach. One of my comrades commented that he felt like he was sitting in a coffin in the bowels of the ship in complete darkness and in complete silence. I believe that we were all thinking the same thing; that we didn't want to be where we were. The thoughts of our families that we might never see again and of the uncertainty of our future hammered away at our nerves synchronizing with the constant thumping of the engines beneath.

We docked in Cádiz at two in the morning and were immediately shifted to a train reminiscent of the cargo holes caked with remnants of the previous four legged inhabitants. They had been used for carrying cattle and now they were transporting us as if we were livestock too. Once we got to the province of Aragón we were housed in shacks with floors covered with straw. Were things looking up?

After twenty five days we were crowded into a dilapidated train which traveled through the night without stops and no lights. We chugged by little villages and streamed through mountain passes until we reached the outskirts of Teruel. The train braked seemingly in the middle of nowhere when they gave orders to abandon the cars of the train as quickly and as quietly as possible.

We were disoriented and confused from the long journey so we literally blindly obeyed the command. We began to run away from the tracks in all different directions in the darkness not seeing where we were going. I vaguely saw some houses in disrepair and I sped toward them to hide behind their fallen walls.

In a matter of minutes and barely 1500 feet away the enemy started firing and all of the railroad cars went up in flames. From the protection of the ruins we looked on in horror as to where we would have been if we hadn't responded to orders instantly. A half an hour earlier and we all would have been wiped out. This was our introduction to the reality of war.

Two months prior to this moment and most of us barely twenty years old, we had left our little island in the Atlantic off the coast of Africa without the slightest notion of what war was really like. None of us belonged to any political party, nor had any affiliation with one. We were all farmers and had never even used a gun. Now we were soldiers far from home in the National Troops plopped down in the worst of the fighting.

They soon gathered us up and set us to marching. I tried to avoid stepping on the bodies of the fallen from the previous day's battle. They had not had time to bury their dead, and a few seemed still to be alive lying there. As the days went on I saw that it was a very common practice to leave the dead and wounded unattended since the need to attend the living was a greater priority. One accepts this truth in the mind, but one can never get accustomed to it in the heart.

The following morning we arrived to "La Muela de Sarrión" in the province of Teruel. There was no shooting when we got there, but we were told to keep patrolling anyway day and night face to face with the enemy trenches. We were able to communicate with the other side by yelling since the distance between the two forces was minimal. The "republicanos" asked us where we were from and when we told them that we were "Canarios", they responded with a sigh and said, "Shit, you are a long way from home. We are willing to declare an unofficial cease fire, if you agree." In the proclaimed neutral zone we mutually shared stories of our lives, of our loved ones, and of our fears.

In a few days the sudden orders came down to commence firing on the enemy and both sides were showered with bullets. Any moans were drowned out by the cracking sound of the discharging rifles. The truce was blown away as if it never had been and I aimed at the face of my friend who now wore the mask of the enemy. The poor man who stuck his head out of the trench was riddled with bullets. Those who remained hunkered down had to drag their fellow soldier, perhaps a friend, off to the side to be able to continue the attack.

The battle lasted three days; three days of hell with no respite, nor sleep. We were then informed by our superiors that the "rojos" had crossed the river and that we were to fall back to Sagunto, Province of Burgos, but they advised us that there were enemy troops there also. Their objective was to control the highways and the railroad in order to cut off supplies to the troops of General Franco. Our mission, as "franquistas", was to prevent them from doing so. The battle of Javalambre in defense of this position was the onset of a long series of skirmishes which would take us into the worst of the fighting, the bloody campaign of the River Ebro. It is recorded in the history books as such.

I am going to limit my telling of the story of my three years in combat. I didn't really know what I was fighting for. I fought for physical survival not political conviction. Many men and women throughout the world have suffered what all we soldiers suffer. Why repeat the tragedies? I will only say as a soldier in the midst of the worst military aggression of our civil war, I saw many a good friend and soldier fall. I got to the point that I avoided to get too close to any of my comrades-in-arms. It became too painful to lose them and too draining on my resolve. Day after day we would throw the bodies into a common grave or leave them abandoned alongside the road as we moved on. I would chant to myself that if I wanted to see my beloved wife again, I would have to survive the depression and dodge the bullets. "I have to survive, she needs me. I have to survive, she needs me." Thinking of Guadalupe kept my illusions alive.

Many times we had to sleep among the dead. It always bothered me that we could not provide a decent burial for these brave men who gave their lives. Sometimes as you marched on you could hear the faint raspy voices of the not yet dead who knew that they were being left behind. The memory accompanied you when they could not and the image of them reaching out to fading backs is still with me today.

I spent most of my war years in the province of Teruel. It snowed a lot in the mountains and the winters were especially cruel. We bedded down on the frozen ground outdoors with no roof overhead. Each solder was issued only one thin cotton blanket. So three soldiers would huddle close together entwined like pretzels so that they could combine the three blankets and make them into one of three layers. There were nights when the snow was so deep that you could hardly move due to its weight pinning you down.

I lost the best years of my life to a war that I did not choose, nor really understand . What were we fighting for? The young men of El Hierro were swept up and strewn onto the battlefields without preparation nor commitment except for that of survival. I am not combative by nature and I have always tried to be a man of peace, coexisting with my neighbors without conflicts.

The "falangistas" (followers of General Franco) abused terribly the men from the Canary Islands. They enjoyed the power that they had and we were greatly afraid of them. They beat all who refused to pick up arms or spoke against Franco. Even sadder yet was the fact that they too were "Canarios".

When the war was over in 1939 soldiers were still needed and I wasn't scheduled to return to my island right away. I learned, however, that a father with more than one son in the military could petition to have one of them released from duty to help at home. My father wanted to obtain the discharge for Toribio my younger brother. Since Toribio had just entered the marines and had not seen any wartime action, I would ask my father to request the release for me instead. I was married, Toribio was not. My wife needed me.

When on leave I went to talk to my father and he told me in no uncertain terms that he would not do it. He reiterated that he did not consider me his son and therefore why should he? In light of his position I went to discuss the problem with my commander. I explained my situation and he replied that I was not to worry, that he would intercede on my behalf. It was determined by my superiors that I merited the discharge in recognition of my military service in the war and the fact that my wife was alone. It was stated in my release papers that "it would be a miscarriage of justice to decide in favor of the other brother." My father, the devout Catholic, never spoke another word to me for the rest of his life. May his God have mercy on his soul.

After I had spent three glorious months back with my wife, history repeated itself. I was called back to active duty and had to serve another four years in the military. Thank Heaven I was stationed in my native Hierro so I could at least see my wife when on leave, but once again I could not assist her with the burden of the farming, or the maintenance of the house, or even helping to carry groceries from town.

During the four years we rarely slept in the barracks since we were to patrol the whole island. We often passed the nights in caves where sometimes we could make the rocky surface a little bit softer by spreading down pine needles and ferns. The mice and spiders were very accommodating and they found themselves "lodging" elsewhere.

The army snatched away seven years of our young lives, negating us the right to be together and to forge our own future. When they finally terminated my tour of duty, I couldn't believe it. I was still fearful that they might reinstate me for a third time. When word came to me that I was going to be discharged for real, I was in a make-shift clinic on the coast suffering from a high fever for which they hadn't ascertained the cause. Consequently, they didn't know how to treat it. The fever would give me nightmares and I would wake up yelling as if I were in the war.

When they told me that I was free to go, I felt better and in four days the fever was gone. I remember the day of our long anticipated reunion so clearly. My wife was waiting for me at the edge of town and in the approaching dusk we walked hand in hand toward our native village as we had done on the night of our elopement. It seemed like an eternity ago and just yesterday simultaneously.

The moment had come for me to be with my wife once again, but also the time had come to confront the bare truth; I needed to find a way to earn a living. After three years of war and another four of army patrols I found myself in the very same situation as before. I had to return to work in the fields and endure the abuses of the "caciques" (the landowners with political clout). So many sacrifices, so much suffering mentally, physically, financially, and for what? Nothing had changed!

Chapter 7
What Was the War For?

Stone house of old

Upon returning home from the war I learned that my father-in-law, Marcelino, had eventually taken his daughter, my wife, back into his household. I knew from a series of new recruits that he had not done so after receiving my letter. He apparently went to look for her in my father's house after the loss of the baby girl. He probably thought with luck I wouldn't come back from the war alive and he would have a built-in servant for many years to come.

Once again I came to claim his daughter as my own, and we left with the hope of living in peace. We knew that the road ahead would be difficult, but we were going to travel its length together and overcome any hurdles side by side. As the years went by we were able to advance little by little with no help from anyone, working hard in whatever opportunities presented themselves. There was a time after the death of the patriarch of the González family that his offsprings tolerated us somewhat better. They occasionally visited us because they saw some advantages in their favor. They used me to cut their hair, to fix their plows, to repair their benches and saddles; to do whatever they couldn't or didn't want to do.

Their behavior was typical of the González gang; put your own benefit above all and to hell with the damage done to others. Just like the father they would approach me with false humility and a hypocritical smile when they needed something. As soon as they got what they were seeking, they would keep their distance and barely say good morning.

So we continued to function on our own. In the 1940's the only source of work on the island was in agriculture. The poor had to live off whatever their meager strip of land could provide for them and their few animals. With luck some might have a cow to give them milk or a goat to allow them to make cheese. However, the price of the cheese was determined by the rich and it was out of reach of the poor man. He could make it, but he couldn't afford not to sell it. He needed every "centavo" to buy his bare necessities.

I remember when one of my godfathers offered me work digging up his potatoes. It would be an all day job from sunrise to sunset, and he would pay me with the leftover leaves to feed my only cow. He considered his proposal a gesture of generosity, but it was a miserly way of getting work done for free, and not even sacrificing a couple of pounds of potatoes from the ones that I would be harvesting. I told him that I couldn't do it due to a previous commitment, but I pretended to be very grateful for the offer for fear of needing something from him in the future. I kept quiet and said nothing of the incident to my wife because I was so embarrassed on behalf of my stingy godfather.

Most of us had to buy the stalks, the leaves, the damaged seeds from the fields of the rich in order to eke out food for our animals, but we didn't have any money to purchase them. So we had to barter, "my labor for your weeds". The rich took advantage of our desperate and dependent situation and would put their animals to graze before selling. The owners received double payment; one for the work by the poor man to clear his fields, and secondly, they benefited from the cheese from the animals they had indirectly fed with a product not worthy of their own livestock. This custom of giving away what you don't want or need and expect a thank you was frequent before the Civil War, but it flourished in the years of great need after the conflict. In 1941 my son was born and it is known as the "year of hunger". So, of course, the less fortunate would accept any little crumb that fell within their reach. The stomach might be indebted, but the mind festered with resentment.

Over the years my wife and I hid many of the incidents of our life from our son. He learned at a very early age that he had no family who cared about him and he witnessed and experienced some of their abuses first hand. The older he grew and the more he came to understand, the greater the animosity he felt. He always said and repeated as a man that he loves the island itself with its abundant natural beauty, but he has no pleasant memories of the people. His happiest moments were enjoying nature away from the human inhabitants. It's impossible to erase the childhood events that form the adult. Our beginnings are our middles and our ends. They are the foundation that character is built upon.

We did not tell our son his grandfather denied us help when we needed it the most, but he observed things and sensed the tension between his elders. This grandfather also mistreated his other children, but not with the intensity shown toward us. As the other landowners did Marcelino set his livestock loose to glean the best of his lands, and then would offer the trampled stems to be sold. If he didn't find a buyer for the torn stalks, he would then, and only then, give the sons-in-law a chance to purchase the dregs.

He treated his relatives by marriage as serfs and showed no consideration for his own blood family members. He would pay you for fourteen hours of hard labor in the sun baked dirt with only a plate of figs, or a few pounds of potatoes including the worms. Why didn't he just pour vinegar on our wounds? It would have been less painful than the humiliation.

When I had retired and my son was established in The United States, I began to open up about some of the things that had happened to us like the episodes mentioned above. He found many of the incidents incredible and unforgivable and he couldn't stop himself from asking, "Why on earth did you two return to an island where the people mistreated you so badly?" I didn't answer him, because I could not come up with a plausible response. I guess I wasn't happy in Venezuela. I didn't know the ropes. I didn't feel that I belonged. Perhaps I didn't want the people of my native island thinking that I was running away as if I were guilty of some wrong doing.

So I continued to divulge my harbored feelings and ease the pressure from within. It was difficult to push out the truth into the light as if a minnow were birthing a whale, but the relief of telling of my woes was mammoth. The moment had arrived to express the anger and the anxiety of so many decades, to explain the exigency of silence that we had deemed so essential. How liberating pending death can be! How an end can be a beginning just in time.

I no longer have to fear the actions of my hidden or declared enemies. Today is the day that I tell the truth, the whole truth, nothing but the truth, so help me God. Let those guilty of inhumanity to me, and others like me, be forced to remove their masks. I do not want to unmask these hypocrites out of revenge. I think that my motivation is to expose them for what they are so that others can see the real malicious beings behind the facade of projected goodness. I guess that I want them to be judged by their peers, so that they will no longer judge me so harshly based on the false testimonials of devious perpetrators. I have tried to be a good, honest, considerate man and they have not. Let the actions speak for themselves.

Someone shared with me once this saying, "It is better to die young than to live all your life on your knees". Perhaps this applies if you are alone, but when you love someone and they depend on you, you don't have the luxury to stand tall against the blows. After spending three years as a soldier in the worst of the battles, I felt that I could surely withstand the excessive abuses by family members and those in power, even if I had to go to my knees once again. I would continue, I thought, to prove myself as a man worthy of respect and eventual acceptance, but this wish was never fulfilled. Even if the leopard changes his spots, he can still bare his teeth and show his claws, so maintain vigilance. The hunt for the prey is constant in the mind of the aggressor and deception is his weapon.

When I returned from the war, I found the same hate grown stronger with age and especially my father-in-law never missed an opportunity to let us know how he felt. He pretended to be a very fair and decent gentleman before the eyes of the outsiders, an image that he did not bother to project at home. He insisted that the townspeople use the title of "don" before his first name which was a sign of respect. He struggled to hide his contempt if they didn't do so. He was autocratic, demanding that things be done his way; vengeful, punishing those who didn't comply with his rules; manipulative, tricking many to do his bidding. When he wanted something from someone, he would approach with smiles and back-slapping, as if you were his best friend or favorite son-in-law. When he got what he was looking for, and no longer needed you, you no longer existed. He never paid back favors unless he would reap some benefit.

His children still manifest the same characteristic behavior of "que viva yo" which roughly translates as ""Me first, and nobody second, third, or fourth." Two of his sons, thinking only of their pockets, and with no regards for their sister's struggle, got together with a brother-in-law to rob us of our savings. They took everything we had in a very difficult time in our life when our need for a helping hand was at its greatest.

To be deceived is bad enough, but it is so much worse when the instigators are from your own family. All the other siblings remained neutral, not one rose up in moral indignation. Yet they continued to come to us if they needed something and then disappeared again until the next time following the González family tradition.

They were like the tide coming in with force and receding with satisfaction. When they were at low tide, they would pass in front of the house without a wave. Once in awhile a sister would stop for a short visit since she had to walk in front of the house to get to the other side where several of her siblings had houses. With hindsight I now suspect that the socials calls were to check up on us and report back to the rest of the family members including the thieves. They enjoyed to hear about our trials and tribulations as if they were watching a TV drama.

Chapter 8
Escape by Sailboat

RAMÓN BARBUZANO MORALES

A Sailboat Called Saturnino

With age the awakening of my senses took place and I reflected on how I could have been so malleable to allow my actions to be shaped by others. Didn't I see that their advice and deeds were directed in their favor and not mine? I had rationalized that my poverty demanded submission. I had always felt, and apparently falsely, that I had to be helpful and obedient and available in order to receive the same consideration from others in the foreseeable future. To have a friend you have to be a friend as the old saying goes. I just didn't realize until way too late that the way of favors is often a one way street. It's like a situation with loaned money; the one who hands over the funds loses sleep and the one accepting the favor often sleeps like a baby.

So here goes the relating of another of my sagas of treachery and mistrust. After the Civil War it was forbidden to leave Spain for a workforce was needed to rebuild the nation, but poverty and hardship still reigned. A rumor started to run rampant throughout the island of El Hierro that it was possible to get rich in a very short period of time in Venezuela. It would only take a week to get there by boat. We, the poor, were mesmerized by the idea. Like those in my same condition of going nowhere we never questioned if it were true, because we all wanted to reach this unreachable dream.

I investigated the possibility for me to emigrate quietly and cautiously, because the undertaking would be illegal. I knew that it would be extremely difficult to leave my wife alone again to defend for herself and now with our son to care for too. The clandestine voyage would be dangerous because one, it was against the law and two, it would be a very risky trip to cross the Atlantic Ocean in a sailboat. I could die as easily in this endeavor as I could have as a soldier in the Civil War. It would be another fight for survival since most of us, who were contemplating this folly, were barely making ends meet.

My brother Toribio, who I never got along with, was part of a group who secretly organized these escape plans. They would buy used boats in Africa at ridiculously low prices because they would require some repairs. Then they would turn around and sell the passages at exorbitant prices to the poor who were driven by desperation. By buying cheap, selling high, and repairing nothing, they would triple their investment in no time. They didn't worry about recuperating their worthless boats. They just wanted to fill them with dreamers and walk away with their money. Whether the gullible believers arrived or not to America was not their concern; out of sight, out of mind.

It wasn't challenging to arrange to be a passenger, since word of mouth in a small village would get you what you wanted. The problem was finding the money. Some signed over their little bit of land as collateral, or they indentured their family members who remained behind. I asked my brother to lend me the amount stipulated. My father, as you know, hated me and Toribio was his favorite out of eight. He had been taught to detest me too. So why was he so willing to advance me the cash? To get rid of me of course. With luck he would never have to see me again. He probably thought that it might even be worth the loss of his "pesetas".

I had no choice but to beg for the financing. It was the only way I could see to accomplish my objective of going to America. Once more out of a fervor to improve my family's lot in life, I stooped to humble myself before a "superior" force. I closed my eyes to the risks and opened my mind to thoughts of riches.

Under the cover of darkness on October 12, 1949 one by one the men began to appear at my house at the very edge of town. On their backs they carried small knapsacks with the barest of necessities for the perilous journey ahead. When all were present, the tearful goodbyes began. We slowly moved away like the ebbing tide leaving behind the sound of weeping which came to us in diminishing waves. The apprehension of never seeing our loved ones again kept thumping in our hearts, matching the rhythm of the heavy plodding tread of our feet, drumming out the refrain, "Don't look back, don't look back, don't look back."

We crept down the steep, almost perpendicular, path of the cliff to the sea from a place known as "El Mirador de las Playas". I know of grown young men in peak physical condition today who stand in awe of what did on that moonless night so long ago. They all say that they wouldn't attempt the descent even in broad daylight with grappling gear.

Because what we were doing was illegal, discovery could be devastating so we maintained silence. Perhaps, like all the others, I dwelled on what was waiting for us: the danger, the uncertainty, the unknown, and the prolonged sadness. Suddenly someone would moan as they hit a rock in the darkness, or curse softly as they stumbled, but the worst was the muffled cry of terror as one of us fell into the abyss and sure death. We wouldn't know who or how many until we reached the bottom. Thank the Lord, we all made it successfully. My imagination had gotten the best of me.

There were 51 of us and 44 were already on the boat. We sailed immediately for Dakar in Africa where four more joined us for a total of 99. Those of us who had left from the top of the island saw the sailboat for the first time as we tumbled unto the shore exhausted. It was old and decrepit and it seemed that it was barely able to stay afloat with its tattered sails and battered hull.

One of the men from my town of San Andrés got so afraid that he refused to get aboard saying, "To sail on that piece of junk is to sail into certain death". This comment to his family when he unexpectedly returned spread like wildfire and the relatives of the committed suffered the flames of worry and doubt. After the projected week's time for the journey to be up everyone with ties to the escapees went to the plazas to meet the bus carrying the mail seeking word of a sailboat named Saturnino. The weeks without word turned into months and soon all hope was lost. Those waiting lamented, "They must have perished at sea."

My nickname is Saturnino and since the sailboat had the very same name I interpreted it as an omen, a good luck charm so to speak. The captain was an old man who believed that he had been hired to take us fishing off the coast of Africa. The story was credible, because food was not abundant after the war.

When he saw so many men, he suspected that something was amiss. We confessed that we intended to go to the Americas and he responded vehemently by stating that he did not have the skills nor knowledge to cross the ocean. He claimed that he had only accepted the job of taking us fishing because he needed the capital to help his daughter out of a worrisome situation. We rose up in what could be labeled a mutiny and wouldn't allow him to abandon the ship. We promised him that we would all pool our resources once there to pay for his passage home. Consequently, he resigned himself and swore to do his best.

The day after our departure the local authorities discovered the absence of almost a hundred men, probably from the loose tongue of the man who stayed behind. The "Guardia Civil", which was and still is the special military police force formed by the dictator Francisco Franco, stormed into the villages. They arrested several women among them my wife to be interrogated as to where their husbands were and who had helped them escape.

My son now had no father (far away), no mother (in jail), and no family (family feuds). I learned later that he went hungry for three days. No one, not even non-family, took in this temporarily orphaned child under their wing, nor under their roof for that matter. At eight years old he slept in the stone "shed" where the tools were kept.

On the second day of being alone hunger drove him to his grandmother's house to ask for something to eat. He found all the aunts and uncles and cousins reunited for a big party with roasted pig and a plethora of side dishes. What a feast for sore eyes and an empty stomach! While everyone was at the table eating the grandmother was making blood sausages. My son told me that he only dared to ask for a few figs and she ignored him, so he pleaded. Without cleaning her hands of the blood and the raw meat she threw a handful of figs at him and said, "Here, now shut up and go away!"

My son has always been stubborn and he knew that his grandparents didn't care a fig for him. So in anger and humiliation he left the figs in the dirt and marched away with his head held high. Next his hunger took him to the house of María whom his Mom considered her best friend. When he reached the house they also were seated in the kitchen enjoying a meal of fish and potatoes. Maria addressed him by saying, "Are you hungry, Eurico?" And she gave him one little new potato on a fork and sent him to sit outside to eat it on the curb next to the dog.

Two days after the arrest of Guadalupe the Guardia Civil returned to our village. One of them (they always traveled in pairs) saw this little boy seated at the base of a stone wall crying softly. It caught his attention and he went to the house of the mayor to find out who this little rag-a-muffin was. The wife of the mayor was the María of one potato on the fork and she and her husband readily identified him. When the officer asked them for the name of the person caring for the boy, they had to confess that no one was.

Children were disciplined by threatening them with the Guardia Civil and accordingly my son was afraid of this man in uniform. With infinite patience he was able to talk to the child and was then inspired to promise him that his mother would be back home the very next day. And he kept his word. Isn't it ironic that the so called boogyman, who was a stranger to him, was the only person who helped a small boy in need when family and friends and townsfolk did not lift a finger?

My wife told me that when they brought her before the judge, the magistrate was surprised to see her last name. He inquired if she knew a certain Toribio Barbuzano and she answered that he was her brother-in-law. The judge just shook his head in disbelief and added, "Toribio and I were having coffee just the other day and he never mentioned that his sister-in-law was being held. If Toribio would have informed me of who you were, you would not have been detained, and your son would not have been left alone to go hungry. You are free to go, Madam. Your son awaits you."

Meanwhile the saga continued at sea. It took us two months to reach land (Brazil) and another month to get to Venezuela. The sailboat had no motor so that we were dependent on sail power. The masts were held in place by ropes and the sails themselves were so tattered from the wind that they were barely functional. With no wind we could not advance. Our "travel agents" were to blame for our miserable conditions and they would be responsible if we were to end up at the bottom of the sea. However, the truth of their treachery would sink with us never to be told.

We had to mend the sails every day. Water was coming in on the starboard side. The ballast, which was for maintaining equilibrium, was made of salt and was being eroded by the waves. The pumps did not have the capacity to displace sufficient water, so someone had to be working the pumps throughout the day and night. We were as disheveled as the boat itself.

The captain turned out to be a noble individual who tried to keep our spirits up even in the most precarious of situations. He apparently didn't hold any resentment toward us and I even think he began to look upon this adventure as his greatest accomplishment in life. In the worst of the howling winds, you would hear his voice with its unique dialect above the din,"No queren ir a Varizuela? Pue, mano a la obra. Asi que vamo entonce a Varizuela!" Loosely translated, "Get your butts in gear, if you want to get to Venezuela".

Finally one night we resigned ourselves to die no matter how much he tried to motivate us. We refused to operate the pumps any longer. It was futile. A hole had developed on the port side and we couldn't keep up with the incoming water. Wiped out and disillusioned we negated to lift a finger since any effort would be in vain. We were doomed.

Two women were traveling with us and one was pregnant with eight months under her belt. When she saw that her fate was sealed, she hugged her husband and shouted, "Hold on to me tight so that we can die together with this our son who we will never see, but who will be with us forever!" So moving were her words that those of us who were able got up to tend the pumps. Those who were too weak to stand whispered encouragement as best they could.

Two days later the wind changed direction and the boat leaned to starboard where less water came in. We were then able to rest and work the pumps only a few hours a day. We had just rationed the little bit of food that we had left when we realized that we were at the mouth of the mighty Amazon. We had arrived to Brazil and we entered the port of Belen. A father and son decided to remain even though they did not speak Portuguese and professed to being so grateful to be on solid ground again. The rest of us chose to continue to Venezuela where we at least would know the language. So after three days with limited supplies bought and minimal repairs made, because that was all we could afford collectively, we set off in the direction of Venezuela.

The weather shifted dramatically for the worse and soon the pumps could no longer handle the quantity of invading water. Our food was practically gone and so was our energy. Once again we collapsed on the deck to docilely await our insistent destiny. We had not seen another ship in all of our journey, so our fate seemed inevitable. A few of the crew members had seen a white splotch on the horizon, but fatigue lowered their heads, and they thought no more about it. It was probably just a gull or whatever.

Suddenly someone realized that it was a big cargo ship and we started to yell and jump up and down, and wave our shirts as flags. The ship kept going and with her any hopes that we might have momentarily had. Then we saw that she was starting a turn toward us and we sank to our knees in exhaustion and in prayers of thanks. Our cheers rose up like thunder and our tears rolled down like gentle rain.

The "New Orleans of the South" was a ship that bore the identity of the flag of The United States. They gave us food, water, and pills for the infections. The captain struggled in limited Spanish to explain to us that Guyana was about 50 miles away from our current position. However, we were welcome to come aboard and he would transport us to safety in The United States.

In light of the short distance according to the captain we decided to try to reach Venezuela since they spoke Spanish there. In The United States the language was English which none of us knew. We calculated that it would only take a couple of days. The American sent some of his crew to repair our pumps and replace our sails. As they returned to the high seas they blew their fog horn in a farewell salute as if to wish us luck.

We reached Guyana in eights days, not two. and we did not encounter any more vessels of any kind. Seven of our group decided to remain in this port, but again the majority opted to go on. There was one thing that I was compelled to do while ashore before leaving and it was imperative. I had to let my wife know that we were okay, but I didn't have any money. So for the first and only time in my life I went begging. I told a man in a little store about our incredible odyssey and explained my situation. He gave me the paper, the pen, the envelope, and the stamp so that I could inform Guadalupe of our arrival to South America. He swore an oath that he would mail it for me the very next day.

My letter would be the very first notification of the sailboat called Saturnino. My wife shared the information with everybody, and she repeatedly had to read it aloud. They came from all over the island just to hear the news for themselves and see the actual paper that it was written on.

Between Guyana and Carúpano in Venezuela we found ourselves in the middle of the worst storm of our trajectory. The waves were maybe thirty feet tall. One of the men aboard injured his leg when the violent rocking of the boat hurled him against the anchor. We were so near, and yet so far. Was it possible that after all that we had endured, we were going to drown off the coast of our final destination?

We had departed from the Canary Islands on October 12, 1949 and we had arrived to Venezuela on January 26, 1950. In spite of the fact that the sailboat was fragile and half destroyed, we reached the mouth of the Orinoco River "limping" but alive. The valiant ship had fulfilled its mission and had carried us to our new home. I couldn't resist to go to see the boat one more time before I left the port. A policeman pointed out the "Saturnino" nestled on her side way in the far back area of the pier. Most was submerged, but part of the main mast was above water and a seagull watched over the remains. I know that it sounds foolish, but I felt as if I were mourning the loss of a dear friend. After all we had spent a lot of time together and we had fought the elements side by side. Rest well my fallen comrade.

    The organizers of these clandestine voyages took advantage of the misery and hunger of their neighbors. Money was the only thing that mattered to them. My brother participated in the purchase of our unserviceable boat. He put in danger the lives of 99 people including me. He permitted the authorities to arrest my wife and caused my son to go hungry. When he found out that I had survived, the first thing that he did was to go to see my wife and demand the money back in full that he had loaned me. With the first meager earnings that I wired home, he appeared to collect. This was the last time that he ever came to my house which was fortunate for my sanity and for his safety.

Chapter 9
The Trunk of the Devil

San Andrés, birthplace of Ramon and Guadalupe

Philosophers say that you can't have good without evil. You have to have a basis of comparison to be able to weigh the validity of your perceptions. On the scale of good versus evil the balance in my life was very lopsided. So many diabolical individuals came to bring us harm and the memories stayed to haunt us for a lifetime. You can't just put these tattered feelings into a trunk and discard them like clothes that have gone out of style.

You should not forget. You don't have to forgive if you take no revenge. Memories are like crude oil that give you the fuel to move forward and not to be stuck in the past. Bad memories give you direction as to where not to go.

I spent ten months in Carúpano, Venezuela working very hard and earning very little. When I was finally able to save up a thousand "bolívares (the currency of Venezuela), I wanted to send them to my wife in the Canary Islands. Since I didn't have a bank account I had hidden the cash in my rented room. I was very good at inventing secret niches for such things. I had seen an advertisement in the newspaper for a company called Financiera Hispana which would wire money to Spain on behalf of the immigrants. So I handed over to them my whole year's savings with such pride in my accomplishment.

I had been taken advantage of so many times in my native land. I faced death repeatedly during the Civil War and while crossing the Atlantic Ocean in a sailboat. Just when I thought that the worst was over and things were looking up for me, I was robbed once again and it was by my own countrymen not the Venezuelans. It was going to be the first money that I was able to send home. They not only took away my wife's reprieve from financial distress, but they undermined my dignity as a husband and a man. Because they were fellow immigrants, it made the disappointment and anger twice as deep. Several days passed under a cloud of depression and disbelief, but then I dragged myself out of bed knowing that I had to start all over. I had no other alternative. I wasn't going to return as a beggar!

Living and working in Venezuela so far from my wife and my son was very trying. Thoughts of her and of the sacrifices that we were both making to get ahead motivated me to keep fighting. I accepted any kind of job that was offered - in agriculture, in construction, loading and unloading trucks of their cargo. I continued to wire my earnings home, but after two years I could no longer endure the loneliness. I crossed the Atlantic, but this time in an ocean liner and away from America toward Europe. Guadalupe had fought her own battles alone for too long. It was time for me to be by her side and for my son to have a father.

Fate took me right back to where I had been two years prior. On one side of the coin (the head) I was extremely happy to be reunited with my immediate family. On the other side of the coin (the tail) it was enormously unpleasant to come in contact with the extended family members. All the negative experiences dealing with them came flooding back. Guadalupe told me about several incidents that had happened to her at their hands while I was so far away. My resentment kept building and building like the continual waves of the tidal surge of a tsunami. I never imagined that there were so many undiscovered facets of maliciousness.

There are certain types of evil in our lives that we can see and perhaps avoid or even confront. However, there are other kinds that are more devastating because we don't know that they exist. Since we don't conceive of the depth of such diabolical plots, we are not adequately prepared for their onslaught.

These hypocritical spectrums enter our houses as friends. They sit at our table and share our food and conversation. They pretend to comfort us in difficult moments and smile graciously in our fortunate times. They manipulate and deceive us for their benefit, not ours. Why we can even develop an affection for these purveyors of false hopes. These fake friends are the worst, because their destructive actions sneak up on you by surprise and its too late to head off the consequences.

Once upon a time...but these are not fairly tales that I relate here. They are of true villains that insinuated themselves into my life, and like the boa tried to squeeze out all they could from their victim, me. Soon after my return home my wife was not feeling well and we had to go to the doctor. She had not slept very much the night before, so we chose to depart early in the morning. It was still dark, but we had a three hour walk one way to reach the capital. After seeing the doctor's assistant, who is assigned to the poor, we started our trek back. Since we couldn't afford to eat in the cafeterias, we had brought something to eat with us. We sat down on a couple of smoothed rocks at the edge of town to share a little bit of cheese and "gofio". (Gofio is toasted wheat flour that can be rolled up into a ball and easily taken with you).

One of my brothers and his wife, who lived nearby in an apartment above their butcher shop, strolled before us on their way home from shopping. They said, "Good morning. How are you?" and continued on to their house around the corner. They knew that we had to be tired after walking so far and that we had another three hours ahead of us. It also had to dawn on them that one of us was sick, because of the effort we had made to come all this way on foot. Yet they didn't even have the decency to offer us a cup of coffee or at least a glass of water. Local custom demanded such a gesture.

In retrospect I now realize that when they were in our village, where they raised their cattle, they demonstrated a certain degree of friendliness. If they needed a favor, they wouldn't hesitate to ask me for it. However, when they were in the capital their attitude toward us flipped over as if someone had thrown the electrical switch to off. We were no longer good enough to associate with their "high class" friends. This is the chameleon behavior so prevalent that I refer to so often.

Another incident even worse in its intent and deception came from the wife of another of my brothers. This woman inhabited a small adobe structure on the edge of our town. She with her little son spent most of her time in our house partaking of our company and our food. She would comment often about how she was afraid to walk back to what she called her "shack" in the dark. The island of El Hierro didn't have electricity in this time period. One day she asked if our son, who was about 11 or 12, could spend the night in their house to allay her apprehensions. We adults agreed, but my son adamantly objected. We won and he was sent.

She offered to feed the two boys dinner since we were doing her a favor by loaning her our son. For more than a year my son was obligated to sleep over in his aunt's house serving apparently as her watch dog. When our son told us that she didn't give him anything to eat for dinner, we didn't believe him. Who on earth would believe that an adult, a family member, would treat a child this way, especially after we had divided equally our groceries with her and her son for the whole previous year. When my son threatened to tell his parents on her, she just laughed and said that they would think that he was just lying to get out of staying with her. It took time and luck to finally discover what my sister-in-law was really like.

Another saga that unfolded happened at the beginning of the summer before my return. My wife had gone down the mountain side to the coast in hopes of finding some fruit still on the trees. My son had asked to go to visit his paternal grandfather, who he rarely had seen because of the distance between us. My wife was hesitant knowing that the grandfather hated the boy's father. Perhaps, she thought, he would show a little more tolerance toward the child he barely knew.

When Eurico (later called Enrique) came back, he was dancing to the clicking of a set of castanets that he said that his grandfather had given him. My wife was moved to tears of happiness at the idea that the old man was mellowing toward them and finally accepting them as relatives. But she was wrong, so very wrong. The castanets were not a present; he had taken them without permission. Maybe he had just wanted to pretend that he had a grandfather who would give him a present like other boys and girls received.

The despotic Eleuterio could not just settle for requesting their return. He wanted to brand the son of his son a thief. He sent an open letter with a neighbor lady that he knew would not be able to resist reading the contents, and of course repeating it. It stated that my wife must hand over the stolen property immediately to the bearer of this epistle, and a childish indiscretion was made public to the delight of the messenger.

My wife punished our son with a heavy heart for she saw that her son realized that he would never have any grandparents. He had suffered abuses, spoken and unspoken, so many times that this was the last straw. The seed of rejection had been planted within and with the passing of the years and the accumulation of experiences the feeling only grew stronger. In fact when we were in Venezuela the other grandfather died and as a teenager he said, "Sorry folks, but he was nothing to me. He always treated me as dirt, so I'm going to the dance anyway. No need to go into mourning. I'm not going to pretend any respect that I don't feel."

Decades later he confided that he had ultimately found himself a grandmother. He borrowed his wife's. She was the first elderly lady who gave him hugs and kisses as if he were her own grandson. This lady of thirteen grandchildren plus the one she unknowingly adopted never knew of the great gift that she had bestowed on my son. Bless you, Ethel May. In comparison the paternal grandfather called him a "savage" because he liked to climb trees and walk on the stone walls rather than the dirt roads. The maternal grandfather would repeatedly say, "Just leave that rebel with me and I'll beat the stubbornness out of him."

There are people, family and non-family, who are cruel by nature and they cause a lot of long term damage. My wife considered a woman called María one of her friends. When I was in Venezuela, my wife had to do everything herself. Sometimes she would leave our eight year old son in María's care so that she could go shopping, or gather fruit, or search for food for the animals.

María had two sons who were a little older than mine. These two made up a game, as they called it, where they told my son that his mother had died and wasn't coming back from the fields. They would then pretend to be the spirit of Guadalupe talking to him from the great beyond imitating a woman's voice. They rolled around on the ground with laughter to see such anguish on the face of the stricken child. What was even worse their mother cackled too at the charade. She didn't put a stop to such maliciousness, that of terrorizing a small boy with the fear of being left alone in the world: no father, no mother, no relatives who cared.

When I came back from Venezuela, these two delinquents could no longer continue that particular game, so they invented another one. They shifted their cruelty to my son's dog, Perruco. They knew that Eurico and Perruco were inseparable. The dog followed him all over. They would capture the dog, tie cans to his tail, and put him in a potato sack. When they set him free, the poor dog would run and run to escape the noise of the cans that were "pursuing" him. Again the giggles were bursting like bubbles into the air at the boy who couldn't overtake his dog to comfort and protect him.

The innocent animal paid the ultimate price with his life. Someone poisoned him. I found him dead and buried him in the orchard without saying a word to my son. In fact I didn't tell a soul. I preferred to let my son think that his dog had run away from the merciless boys than to imagine his four legged friend in the throws of a painful death.

I always had the feeling that the dog was poisoned by the two pranksters who were so sadistic in their play. I never had any proof so I accused no one. However, thirty years later one of the boys, then a man, came for a visit to the islands from Venezuela. My son was also there from The United States. We stared reminiscing about the old days over a couple of glasses of wine.

The culprit couldn't withstand the temptation to inquire about the dog, to ask if we ever had ascertained who poisoned it. I had already confessed to my son, so he knew of his pet's demise. Still laughing after all these years, he imitated the voice of the small boy running after his dog, calling out "Perruco, Peruco". My son and I both knew at that moment that we had discovered the identity of the dog poisoner. And the party was over. We made excuses to obligate him to leave. Tsk, tsk. We never saw him again.

After living in the smallest of the Canary Islands and wearying of the abundant abuses by family and friends, we decided to try our luck in the bigger island of Tenerife. With our savings from Venezuela we bought a little store in the capital city of Santa Cruz. At the end of our first year we were doing okay, but not really well; just making ends meet, but no headway to speak of. Therefore, we voluntarily reverted to our old life on the remotest island. We would be able to cut down on our expenses by growing our own food on account of having the land free and clear.

It was at this time that my brother, the husband of the women who we helped in his absence, unexpectedly appeared from America with a plan to return with his family. He suggested that we go with him. We could all travel together and once in Venezuela he promised us that we could stay in his house until we got established. He added that he was grateful for the way that we had aided his wife and son when he was far away and he intended to pay the favor back. With this moral and financial safety net, we elected to go for it.

I went to Tenerife to arrange for the required documentation to immigrate and Guadalupe began to pack the trunks. My wife had always been very religious and she felt compelled to fulfill a promise that she had made to the patron saint of the island, "La Virgen de los Reyes". She wanted to thank "Her" for protecting me during the crossing of the Atlantic in the sailboat. By the way I had taken a picture of "Her" with me to the Civil War and I also was indebted.

The gesture of thanksgiving consisted of walking barefoot with lightweight clothing in the damp and windy winter weather for about ten miles downhill. She would then undergo the night on her knees praying in the sanctuary dimly lit with candles. The next day she would return walking up hill under the same circumstances.

My son would have to once again bed down in the house of the aunt who allegedly didn't give him any dinner for months on end. When my wife arrived home from her personal mission, she located our son asleep in our storage shed on top of the hay. He claimed that his aunt didn't want him around this time, because she desired to be with her husband, if you get my drift. My son explained that the two of them were arguing so as to whether the kid should stay or go, that he just got off his mattress on the floor and left. Neither of them tried to stop him.

The following day we heard their version, "We tried to prevent him from leaving, but you know how stubborn your son can be". And as was the case with the missing food, we believed them not our son.

For our trip to Venezuela Guadalupe made four "quesos de almendras". These are like candy with real almonds that when cooked are shaped into rounded cheese form about the size of a large cottage cheese container. They take a lot of work stirring and a lot of almonds purchased. My wife gave two to our sister-in-law and we initiated the voyage across the sea by sharing ours. When all six of us (two couples and two kids) demolished our supply, the party was over, no more dividing of the treats.

Once we were all set up in their house in Caracas, and several days had passed, my thirteen year old son came running. He had spied his aunt giving his cousin some of the almond candy, that supposedly was all gone, while he hid behind the tree in the courtyard eating a generous chunk. We went to see for ourselves to put to rest these endless tall tales. We took her by surprise and saw that she truly was capable of concealing food from us to give to her son. My son had been telling the truth about her not providing him with any dinner. She gave a new meaning to the expression self-centered; for her everything was one sided - take, take, take, but never give. Ironically years later both of her sons developed serious health problems related to obesity.

The incident of the hidden food occurred approximately three weeks after getting to South America. My wife demanded that we move out and I concurred. Luckily I was able to rent a room in a big house that had been subdivided for the immigrant sector. A family had a private bedroom, but the kitchen, bathrooms, and sitting room were all common ground. An acquaintance from work vouched for us and the owner agreed to wait until the end of the month for the rent money.

We lost contact with my brother and his wife. I worked in the farmers' market and my wife took in laundry to be washed by hand. My son picked up the laundry to be washed and delivered the packages with the clean and ironed clothes. A year later out of the blue my brother knocked on the door with a tragic story. His wife was mentally ill due to the birth of their second child. Because of this postpartum depression she couldn't be trusted with the infant. He begged us to care for his little son. My wife couldn't refuse for as she said the baby was not at fault.

The child was with us for seven months and the parents rarely came to see him. When they did stop by, the mother remained outside! Then one day they appeared to claim their son and took him away without even a thank you. It was tear jerking for my wife to see the baby go. She had become very fond of the little guy.

Things are not always as they seem to be on the surface and this incident turned out to be a farce. Many years later my sister-in-law confessed in a moment with her guard down that she had pretended to be crazy. She just didn't want the job of caring for a newly born with dirty diapers and sleepless nights.

Once again and again and again she thought only of herself. If her husband was worried, too bad. If her sister-in-law had a tremendous work load with the laundry business and a small infant, who cares? She probably reflected, "I'm smart. They're dumb. I win".

You know soap operas never seem to end, Years go by and the diva comes aknocking to make another one of her dramatic entrances. She has had a big fight with her husband and she announces that she will be lodging with us. She rants and raves that if she doesn't get her way, she'll just recreate her famous act of the demented woman. Manipulation via lies was her modus operandi and her preferred method of solving all of her problems. It didn't matter to her one iota if she were causing complications for others. In her mind she was the center of the universe and all of the people on the planet should orbit around her. My stars, what an ego!

My son said that he never understood why we returned to the island where so many treated us so badly. By allowing people to continually take advantage of our good nature, we were indirectly responsible for some of our problems. I couldn't give him a straight answer at the time, but as I thought about it, I think that we wanted to avoid possible confrontations. We never knew when we might need something from someone. Therefore, we felt that we had to close our eyes to certain things and maintain silence. If not, we might make things worse. I suppose that we were constantly searching for affection and/or approval trying to recuperate family or find some kind of friends. I now know at 96 years of age that all was in vain and I will die disillusioned. One can not expect respect, even if it's merited.

I now wish that I could have been more like my son contrary to the old days when I wanted him to be more like me. He learned long ago that he didn't have any family who cared for him as a person. People do not take advantage of him, because he doesn't give second chances. He detests hypocrisy. He respect only two qualities: Truth, don't lie to me and honesty, don't steal from me. He doesn't trust people until they prove otherwise. Most do it the other way around. At one time I wanted him to come to live in the Canary Islands to be close to us. Today I am very, very glad that he didn't heed my wishes. He is acclimated to The United States and is free from the ties that bound him through me. I am "Herreño". He is not.

As I pondered over his comment about why we returned, the memories of the abuses passed through my mind like looking at old movies on the TV screen. Three brothers-in-law got together to rob me of my money in Venezuela. Another used my flat roof as a repair shop for his farm implements and of course damaged it. Another in-law claimed that a man who rented one of my houses left the island owing three months rent. Yet this relative, who was overseeing my properties in my absence, got his entire house wired for electricity at the cost of the equivalent amount of three months rent. Oh, did I mention that the "fly-by-night" renter was an electrician by trade?

A niece who was newly married asked to live in one of our houses. We didn't want to do it to avoid possible conflicts with family members as had been our past history repeatedly. The father implored and promised that he would be responsible for any expenditures that his daughter might be unable to keep up with. After six months she got behind in the rent, but we didn't press the matter. We wanted to help her get on her feet financially.

Then one night under the cover of darkness the couple left not only owing several months rent, but also leaving behind exorbitant unpaid electric and water bills. We approached the father, my wife's brother, and said that we would absorb the missing rent money, but would appreciate it if he would take care of the outstanding water and electric balances that were due. His response? Not a word spoken then, nor for the rest of his life.

The brother-in-law with the brightly lit house also stopped talking to us. He appealed to us to put up as collateral one of our houses so that he could invest in establishing a banana plantation. I replied in the negative, stating that I had gotten burned too often by family members. Why didn't he ask for a loan from his brother who robbed us and with whom he got along so well? I suspect that since the venture could be risky, all of the brothers voted for me, Saturnino, to take the loss if the enterprise should fall through.

    P.S. The banana crop dried up and the funds withered away. My God, what is worse, a selfish and uncaring family, or no family at all?!

Chapter 10
Venezuela, Land of Hope

The family immigrates

When I think of Venezuela, good and bad memories come to mind. It was the beginning of a new chapter in our life, full of hope and determination. We were together and ready to confront the hurdles toward a better economic situation. After barely a month in a foreign country all three of us were working. My wife took in laundry, my son did the pick up and return of the clothes, and I labored in the farmers' market. My wife and I, however, never lost thoughts of our homeland and of the dream to return.

One day I noticed that my son seemed to be changing; more confident, more independent, and more anti-herreño.

He had met a gentleman who worked in Radio Caracas Televisión. The station was not far from where we lived, so he passed by practically every day making his deliveries. When the man asked him why he went by so often, he answered that his mother took in laundry, and the TV director responded that he would like to become one of her customers.

When the other employees saw the young boy of thirteen so frequently, they asked their boss about his identity. He in a whimsical moment replied that the lad was his son since he had no children of his own. Consequently, my son was given free rein of the studio as long as he did not get in their way.

I now realize that this experience opened his eyes to new ideas because he encountered a variety of people not from the Canary Islands with different points of view. Sometimes he would be an extra in a program and they would pay him. What a surprise and a thrill for him to have money of his own. While Enrique was exploring Caracas with gusto and curiosity and absorbing the Venezuelan culture, my wife and I continued to work and socialize with our "paisanos", the other immigrants from El Hierro.

Our life went forward unlike the life that we had left behind that was going nowhere. Quite a few of those who traveled with us on the ship to Venezuela were unable adapt to the new environment. Within the first year they went back perhaps humiliated, but definitely without the riches that they had anticipated attaining.

Guadalupe liked Venezuela and my son loved the adventure, the newness, and the release from his oppressive roots. I, like my countrymen, never really adjusted, but the desire to reach economic stability was the driving force that gave me the strength to continue. My goal was to accumulate a nest egg to take back to Spain. It was never my plan to stay in America.

Soon the herreños began classifying my son as "acriollado" which was a derogatory term for someone who embraced the Venezuelan ways as if he were guilty of treason. These comments only accomplished in pushing him further away from his native culture and exponentially contributed to creating a greater gap between us too.

At fourteen years of age Enrique freely roamed all over the metropolis of Caracas. After working a short time in the market alongside his fellow "canarios" he found employment in a travel agency. It wasn't a desk job which would not have suited him. He was assigned the task of arranging for travel documents for their clients which led him to deal in person with the personnel of the embassies, the port authorities, the airport, and various government offices. This position in the agency put him in contact with a multitude of people so unlike the ones with whom he grew up. These individuals unknowingly drew him further and further away from his background.

Meanwhile my wife and I worked diligently, sometimes into the night, but we always had our hearts set on going home. After almost ten years I finally was able to go back alone with the purpose of buying a house in the island of Tenerife so that we would have a place to live when the time came to return. I found a colonial style one centrally located and even with a little store attached. I chose this particular dwelling thinking that my son would be able to earn a living from this space either as a store site or for office space. Even at fifteen he had other plans and I should have suspected it. He abhorred everything herreño and embraced anything that was not.

My son and I had heated arguments due to the critical comments and false accusation of the herreños. Our conflicts reached such extremes that he refused to participate in any of the social events in the club called "La Casa Canaria". As was the custom among many immigrant parents, they would send their sons back to the hands of females relatives who were charged with the task of finding a suitable young girl for him to marry. Through these marriage ties the young men living abroad would be lured to the homeland.

When we suggested he take a nice little trip to the Canary Islands for a nice little vacation, he detected the ruse. He saw right away that we were up to matchmaking. His explosive reaction rained down on us like confetti. He stated adamantly that he would not go, that he would never marry, nor even date an herreña woman. Any woman that he proposed to would be of his choice and nobody else's.

He deliberately cut ties with the islanders in Venezuela. He became a member of the "Centro Asturiano de Caracas". He learned the dialect and the dances of this province of northern Spain, and understandably at sixteen his first girlfriend was "asturiana". Because they were very young talk of marriage was a far distant and remote notion that might never come to be. Since their relationship was not at this stage, custom did not require that he bring her home to meet his parents. Therefore, we were never introduced. The gossips, however, kept us informed. They told us that they were such a handsome couple and it was such a sight to see how beautifully they danced together. Our daily lives followed different paths and we learned of our son's activities through third parties. He was drifting away as we stayed anchored in our past.

When my son was a boy, we did not believe him. It was easy for me to find fault in what he said, but he had to accept whatever I said. After all I was his father and the head of the household. Today at more than 90 years old it occurred to me that by not believing him, unconsciously I was labeling him as a liar. I now know that many of the times when I did not give credence to his denials, he was in fact telling the truth.

The only excuse or explanation that I have is that in those days I just couldn't conceive of such cruelty in others and especially when the act was directed toward an innocent child. Even today I still can not wrap my mind around the idea that there are some people who calculate their lies to purposely create problems. There are those who invent gossip and intentionally spread it around as if it were a game for their personal amusement. One thinks that it is sort of normal for a kid to tell untruths, but for an adult to do so and on such a large scale is unforgivable. No wonder my son feels nothing but contempt for these recreational child abusers.

Little by little the young boy was becoming a man and often times the parents are the last to notice. The resentment was festering from all the false accusations and then a couple of incidents took place which would change our relationship forever. My son was fourteen and an herreño blamed him for the theft of a radio antenna that was off an old junk car that he had set aside for parts. As a bachelor he was living with my son's godfather and another relative with a son about the same age as mine.

This man sent me a message that he wanted to talk to me face to face. When we met, he claimed that my son was a thief and what was I going to do about it. Having been an honest man all of my life with temptation surrounding me in my poverty, I could not abide by the idea of having a son who was not. So great was my anger that I hurried home to confront the culprit. He swore that he hadn't stolen the antenna and once more I did not believe him. Blind with rage

I took my belt off to teach him a needed lesson. He continued yelling to profess his innocence and I kept on swinging. Finally my wife intervened and separated us.

Several days later the accuser came to confess that he had found the antenna hidden among his godson's belongings and that he wanted to apologize to me. There was no mention of an apology to my son on his behalf. What a great injustice for such an insignificant thing!

I turned my back on him without a word and went to ask my son for his forgiveness. I explained what had happened. Because my remorse was so deep I promised never to lift a finger to him again, but it was too late. This time I had not punished the boy, I had angered the man within. The damage was done. The bitterness toward me and all my unfair actions were way too ingrained. From that day forward the transformation in my son was dramatic. He became more distant and more rebellious and spent more time outside the house.

Then things deteriorated even more due to a denigrating and shameful event which marked his final retreat. The drama began in a pleasant park outside Caracas called "El Junquito". The teenage girls from the boarding house where we were living had organized a picnic in the countryside for all of us. In order to understand the intensity of the upcoming scene a little bit of background on the main characters is required.

One of my wife's sisters lived in the same boarding house as we did with her four children. Since her husband had abandoned her for another woman my nieces and nephew didn't have a father present. So I tried to be their surrogate father. The expression "buen tío" in Spanish means "a good guy", but it can also mean literally "a good uncle".

When my son said that his father was a "buen tío", people thought that he was praising me. We both knew that he was referring to my faults as his father and my efforts to be a good "father" to his cousins.

During the festivities my son and the oldest girl, who was also teenager, got talking and wandered off to get away from the noise. They were fond of each other because they had grown up together. My son being a few years older felt protective of her. He never allowed any young man to be disrespectful toward her. After awhile they returned to the party and my son left to go to see his girlfriend in the city.

My sister-in-law and her ex-husband, who happened to be making one of his rare visits, accused their daughter and my son of having had sex in the bushes during their brief absence from the party. A scene was made in front of everybody and the drama continued full force back at the boarding house with yelling and screaming and sobbing.

Act 3 - My son enters the scenario into a real farcical soap opera without having an inkling of what has preceded his arrival on "stage". The father of the "violated girl" planted himself in front of my son and threw the accusation in his face. My son gave him a look full of hatred and said not a word controlling himself unlike all the others. He turned to his cousin who ran to him in tears saying that they wouldn't believe her that nothing had happened between the two of them. The females; the mother, my wife, the aunts, were all insistent that they would have to get married.

Final curtain - The two teenage cousins hugged for the last time ever, and their friendship died. My son swore that he would not have contact with his cousin anymore so that she could avoid any further problems. The "hero" of the play rode off into the sunset, or to put it real terms, soon after my son left for The United States. Wow, when he keeps his distance, he keeps his distance!

My niece must have felt trapped in her repressive and unpredictable environment. She went on to have three disastrous romantic liaisons. She fell in love with a married man who broke off with her to reunite with his wife. The second man was Italian and she left him practically at the alter, because she had changed her mind. The day before her next pending marriage the groom was arrested on the way to the church for armed robbery. In the end she married the first man when he decamped leaving his wife and child and came looking for her.

Many years later her mother, the sister-in-law, confessed that she had invented the story of her daughter's and her nephew's sexual misconduct. The purpose of her plan was to get her husband back. She thought that if she could only convince him that their daughter needed a father to protect her, he'd return to her. Once again an herreña woman only considered herself and she used the common weapon of the wagging tongue to achieve what was to her benefit alone.

Many were the times in my life when I believed that there were good, honest, considerate people in the world, but repeated heart-wrenching, despicable events have soured my soul. After having lived almost a century I am convinced that evil is an incurable malady. It is impossible to change people. Only if the individual truly wants to improve himself, can he create his own metamorphosis. I have changed and with this book the new true me has emerged from its cocoon.

Ironically I have accomplished this internal rearranging with the help of my son, although he doesn't know it. Many comment that my son is very deep in his philosophical observations and often offers some very wise insights. For example, when one of his aunts came to see me and ask for my forgiveness for the problems that she had caused me, Enrique said, "Diabolical people do not have moments of remorse, only moments of weakness". He was right. Said aunt by her consequent behavior proved him to be correct. She had not changed neither inside nor out.

It took me a long time to accept my son's way of thinking. To be honest there were many a time when his verbal responses to my problems irritated me. When we permitted "family and friends" (quote, unquote) to treat us badly and say nothing, his retort would be, "Don't you realize that by receiving these abuses in silence, you are just cultivating the opportunities for them to take advantage of you over and over again?" Often he had just the right proverb for the occasion like Sancho Panza of literary fame, "He who wants to die, finds the thought of death glorious."

In contrast to my personality my son never hid his distain for his extended family. Today I understand his feelings, but in the past his attitude was embarrassing. My wife and I tried to advise him to control his temper and his tongue and to maintain a decorum of respectability through silence. Over the years we had kept secret many of the things that had happened to us or were said to us. We didn't want to stoke the fire of resentment inside of him in fear that his train of thoughts would run away with him and put him on a collision course with danger from those who didn't like what he said.

The multitude of deceptions we had suffered slowly reshaped our way of thinking. I, more than my wife, finally had to speak out to alleviate the pressure of the spiritual miasma within me. In a way it was better that we had kept things from our son's awareness. He had endured enough abuses of his own by the mere fact that he was our offspring. He didn't need us to add our burdens to his.

My daughter-in-law once asked me why the herreños were so critical of her husband and I couldn't come up with an explanation. At that time in my life I actually wished that my son were more herreño. On several occasions I reprimanded him for expressing his strong opinions and suggested that he keep them to himself to avoid problems; in other words to shut up. I guess that I wanted him to be like me; to be silent and to try to get along with everybody. With hindsight I am so glad that he didn't heed my advice. His strong character was his escape valve. Sometimes out of bad comes good.

After having been in the nursing home for awhile I was able to see my son through the eyes of others. When he came to the island of El Hierro all the way from The United States, he would visit my wife and me every day during his stay. Frequently he would drop in twice a day and always for two or three hours at a time. So many of my companions in the "residencia", who showed up at the same time, would get to spend time with my son too. They got to know him. Our "new friends" saw Enrique as he was, not as our "old friends" portrayed him. The new admired him; the old were jealous of him. They were envious of the barefoot boy who grew up in poverty and yet became rich by their standards. They resented his harmonious marriage, his healthy demeanor, and his obvious intelligence.

He once told me that The United States is not a paradise, as no country is perfect, but America gave him a great gift - his self esteem. The Americans encouraged him to be whatever he wanted to be and helped him to pass the tests that allowed him to enter the university. The herreños constantly discouraged him by undermining any objective that he might have had. I am delighted that he is living where he wants to be and with the woman of his choice. Remember we tried to choose a wife for him? I wouldn't trade my daughter-in-law for any other because she understands my son as I never had. I now comprehend and approve of his intention to never return to the Canary Islands to live. It was the right decision for him.

Chapter 11
The Son Leaves Home

ENGLISH LANGUAGE CENTER
FALL 1965   MICHIGAN STATE UNIVERSITY

Michigan State University
*Note - Enrique Barbuzano Gonzalez, first row, ninth from the left, sweater with V stripe

In Venezuela my son had opportunities to see alternative possibilities to those of the limited herreños' vision and his manner of thinking changed accordingly. He adopted the culture of this new country because it was different and discarded the ways of the old country of his birth. He made Venezuelan friends and he went anywhere in the capital without reservation. He was entranced with the rhythm of the music of the Caribbean and he distanced himself from the repetitive chirping of the Canary Island flute (his words, not mine). He refused to attend any cultural event presented by the Canary Island colony in Caracas.

We were now moving in two different worlds and the following incident showed me how true this statement was. Due to a fight that broke out in the farmers' market the police arrested me along with several others. I had never been in jail and the worst of it was the shame that I felt, as much for my wife as for me. We didn't know anyone who could help us and I found myself at the mercy of an unknown justice system.

After a couple of days they came to tell me that I was free to go. They added that General So and So had intervened on my behalf and that his personal escort team would take me home. I told them that it was a mistake, that I did not know such a person, thinking that I would just be returned to my cell once he saw me. He probably had me confused with someone else. The guards just laughed and said, "Hurry up. The general doesn't like to be kept waiting."

They accompanied me to the street where indeed a military car was idling right in front of the main entrance. The aides on the motorcycles cleared the traffic for us to pass. Imagine the awe with which the neighbors witnessed the scene. After he shook my son's hand and left saying that he was glad to have been of service, I turned to my son in shock. He explained that he was friends with the General's son. At that moment I was pleased that my son was "acriollado".

It dawned on me that my son's job in the travel agency also afforded him with many contacts outside my circle of acquaintances. When he was arranging for certain documents for their clients he was dealing with a variety of people from the porters at the doors to the executives behind the desks. Since he liked his work and he preferred to be on the move, rather than be stuck in the confines of four walls, he was happy. I'm sure this attitude shone through when dealing with people.

I was pleasantly surprised that he knew so many "important" individuals, but my wife and I were bowled over when he came home one day to announce that he was going to The United States to study English. He had already obtained a student visa and a scholarship from the American Embassy. At seventeen he was enrolled at Michigan State University in the city of East Lansing, state of Michigan for the next term. It was a done deal, no room for discussion.

We tried to dissuade him by pointing out that he would be going to a strange country, far from help from us if he were to need it, and he didn't even speak the language. The advice came too late because his plan was premeditated. Sneaky devil! I guess he learned something from his old man after all. He was determined to find something better in his life, and now, not then, I believe that it was the best decision that he ever made.

With this action he was able to break free of the suffocating ties to his country men. In addition he escaped from the parents who did not have the capacity to understand his restlessness. We experienced sadness and relief at the same time; sad that we might lose our only son and relief in the hope that he might find in The United States whatever it was that he was searching for to calm his unsettled soul.

Once in Michigan he wrote to us frequently relating things about his new life. The scholarship that he had been awarded included room and board, but it also required that he work on campus part time to cover the cost of tuition, books, and have some leftover for personal expenses. According to him he would work at whatever job was offered; painting, repairing roofs, cleaning offices. He had quite a few bosses over the several years when he was a student, and not one mistreated him. Most were especially kind.

He told us of one foreman in particular that he said that he would never forget. This man had two sons who were also studying at the university. So he understood Enrique's need to work yet have time to study. He would drive my son to the job site and would inform at what time he would be coming back to pick him up. This boss knew how long the job would take to complete, but he always added a couple more hours so that there was time to hit the books, or even take a little nap. When one job would end, this gentleman would already have lined up another for him.

The students with scholarships were only allowed to accept part time jobs on campus. They also had to continue their classes. The summer months were, however, a time when these students could work full time without enrolling in any academics. The man mentioned above had a friend who had been awarded the contract to paint all of the dormitory rooms in all of the buildings of the university. With over a student population of 50,000 this represented plenty of work. My son would be earning three times the amount ordinarily received, thus enabling him to pay for all of his courses for all of the following year.

When the fall term began the new foreman offered him a full time, permanent job with his company. Enrique thanked him profusely, but clarified that he wanted to finish his studies. The man responded by saying that he looked forward to at least having him on his crew the following summer.

My son had hidden from us quite a few things that had happened to him while he was away. When he returned to Venezuela for a short visit, he shared the details of perhaps the scariest moment in his young life. Three days after reaching the university and settling in, he was not feeling very well. He left the dorm to find the nearest medical hospital. Some students found him unconscious in the snow. They called for an ambulance that transported him to the university clinic. Since he knew very little English, next to none, he was unable to communicate with the doctors and staff. He didn't comprehend what they were saying and he couldn't describe his symptoms, nor answer any of their questions.

The personnel of the clinic put fliers all over campus, "Urgent - translator Spanish/English needed for recent arrival from Venezuela - contact clinic." My son swears that he will always remember that moment when the Guatemalan young man entered his room speaking Spanish. His joy and relief were so great that he didn't even bother to wipe away the tears.

The doctors put him isolation not knowing what the illness was and whether it were contagious or not. They kept him for two weeks of observation and then released him since his condition seemed to have cleared. Two years later while in South America he had to have emergency surgery to prevent his appendix from bursting. Maybe the two illness were related, who knows?

Via his letters he would describe all the interesting people that he had met, many of them from a great variety of different countries. He felt as if he had learned as much from them outside the classroom as he had from the instructors inside the classroom. He found their unique customs and mentalities eye opening. As his world expanded our world must have seemed to him very small indeed as if he were looking through a telescope in reverse. Among his friends with whom he regularly ate in the cafeteria were an American, a Nigerian, a Chinese-American, and a Canadian.

He also recapped for us his most difficult moment; the day that he received a letter from his girlfriend informing him long distance that she was breaking up with him. I then disclosed that she had come to the boarding house where we rented a room to ask about him. She had never met us and my son wrote her every day, so we both agreed that it was just a pretext on her part. When she saw our limited financial situation, it was probably the motivating factor for her to pen her "Dear John" communique. We being in Venezuela learned through the proverbial grapevine that she soon had another young man to escort her to all the social events that she adored.

Almost a year later Enrique came to Venezuela to divulge his intentions to marry an American girl if she would accept him. But first he wanted her to come to meet his parents and see his circumstances for herself. He chose to be honest and open with this young lady from the very beginning so as to avoid a possible repeat of the incident with the ex-girlfriend.

My wife and I, of course, were disappointed. We implored, "Are you sure that you know what you're doing? She's from a different culture, speaks a different language, and isn't even Catholic." We had always hoped that our only son would marry a girl from El Hierro or at least from Spain. We were mortified to think that she might not even speak Spanish. Today I am grateful to my daughter-in-law. She understands my son like we never did, and she makes him happy. She is not demanding in a high maintenance sort of way and she has always treated us with respect and consideration.

Before asking Elizabeth to marry him, he came back to Venezuela specifically to contact his old girlfriend. They had never really spoken about what had happened between them and my son wanted to clear the air. He confessed that he sought an explanation for her behavior and that he was seeking closure. He wanted to start his new relationship with a clear conscience and an empty heart ready to be filled anew.

Soon after he invited his "true love" to come to Caracas and they got engaged with our blessing. Of course we would give them our blessing, because it was something that we never received from our parents and we would not inflict the same on our son. When he asked Dr. Powell, his future father-in-law, for his daughter's hand in marriage, he also gave them his blessing. He added that my son had better take very good care of his daughter, or he would chase him down over the Andes, up the Amazon, around Cape Horn, in a professorial way of speaking, of course.

They got married in Michigan and we were unable to attend the ceremony due to limited funds. However, they planned to come to live in Venezuela so we were delighted. We rationalized that we missed out on one event in their lives, but we would have them nearby for years to come.

When they were able to make arrangements to move to South America, my daughter-in-law was pregnant with our first grandchild, but it was not to be. We were all together when the big earthquake of 1967 hit Caracas. Apparently running down four flights of stairs from the apartment to the street to escape the falling debris caused the umbilical cord to twist. Several months later nature aborted the little girl who was going to be named Laura Alicia.

The city was in total chaos and my two children were obligated by circumstances to move in with a married cousin. Her husband had left the first wife supposedly because he had difficulty accepting the fact that his daughter from this previous union was slightly mentally retarded. My niece showed her true colors following in the family footsteps of selfishness by putting her own benefit above all others. The cousin tried to dominate and intimidate my son's wife, and although she was stoic, she was not dumb. Elizabeth did not want to present her husband with more problems when he got home from a long day working on one of the rescue crews from after the earthquake. To uncover bodies, some dead, some barely alive was trying enough.

My son wasn't aware that his new wife spent her days in the bedroom, knowing that the two cousins didn't want interruptions from an outsider in their daily lives. A few times they went on a picnic without inviting her, yet left hardly any food behind in the refrigerator. One evening when my son arrived to the shared apartment, he found his wife gently crying and she told him what happened. She overheard through the closed door of the bedroom the happy laughter and the popping of a cork from a champagne bottle.

My niece and her husband were celebrating the death of his handicapped daughter because they no longer would have to pay child support. My "daughter" said that she was crying for the child that they didn't want and crying for the baby she did want and lost. Of course, it was impossible to remain there any longer, but it was difficult to locate housing due to the recent tremor.

Over 8000 people lost their lives in that fateful earthquake and many buildings were structurally damaged. Luckily my son and I stumbled upon an unfinished apartment in a not so good section of town. We snatched it up and finished the work ourselves. We put in the windows, installed the bathroom fixtures, and hung the doors. Bless my daughter-in-law for when she first saw it she commented, "Wow, the first home of our own and right above a bakery with the heavenly smell of fresh baked bread". To reassure her my son said, "And don't worry, dear, about the thieves, the pimps, and the drug dealers here in Cuatro Vientos, we're safe. They'll just think that we are one of them and leave us alone."

How did we know that my daughter-in-law was telling the truth or that she was perhaps exaggerating? One, my son found the empty champagne bottle in the trash bin. Two, my son had just paid the cousins his share of the grocery bill and my wife and I peered into the refrigerator to see that the shelves were bare. Three, on the day after market day my son and his wife came to spend some time with us in the boarding house. Elizabeth, who was never a hearty eater, consumed three pork chops along with all of the side dishes practically scraping off the design on the plate.

Soon after all this his cousins called my son aside to clarify that they didn't have a problem with him, only with his wife. He responded without hesitation, "Anyone who has a problem with my wife, has a problem with me." These were the last words spoken between them.

About fifteen years later this cousin found her husband dead in his bed. He had gone to sleep and didn't wake up and he was only in his forties. A few years later she was diagnosed with cancer. One day from Michigan it occurred to my son to telephone this cousin. Even today he can't explain why he thought of her out of the blue after so many years had gone by. They talked briefly on telephone and he remarked, "I am going to be coming to Venezuela next month and if you like I could stop in for a visit," not knowing that she was terminally ill. She responded with these words, "Yes, I would like that very much." When he arrived she was gone. She had died the week before and she also was in her forties. And we, my son, my wife, and I, didn't drink champagne.

After the famous earthquake of an intensity of 8.6 on the Richter Scale many of us had to start over; to look for a new job or to raise up the devastated one from the rubble. Customer contacts collapsed, factories fell, people scattered, and so my children did too. They decided to return to The United States. My son requested that we not tell anyone that they had left the country, and if anyone should ask, to not give out any information. Why? because my son was fed up with the treacherous family members and the hypocritical friends.

When my son almost died from a "ready to burst at any minute" appendix not one of his friends came to see him. The mother of the niece, who celebrated the death of the child, organized a boycott to prevent visitors from appearing in the hospital. I guess it was in support of her daughter's claim that Enrique and Elizabeth were ingrates after all they had done allowing them to stay in their apartment.

By going to The United States to live permanently he was closing the door to his past. He was distancing himself from his native land, its inhabitants, and their culture. The chapters on Venezuela, the Canary Islands, and even Spain were ended. His future would take a very different turn and ours too.

Since Enrique would no longer be in Venezuela why should we remain? We initiated our preparations to migrate home, to the mother country of our yearning. We had a house waiting for us in Tenerife. Ironically my son's decision to leave Venezuela facilitated our choice to abandon America and embrace Spain once again. We thought that the best years of our life were about to commence and hopefully for my son too.

Chapter 12
Returning Home

The house then and now in Santa Cruz de Tenerife

In the summer of 1970 we went to Michigan to see our one year old grandson for the first time and then to continue on to Spain from The United States. We had spent almost twenty years away from our homeland and we were understandably very excited with anticipation.

My wife, Guadalupe, had never seen the house that I had bought for us several years prior. I had left the key with a cousin of mine so that she could check on the house and clean it every once in awhile until we came back. Finally we would be able to enjoy the fruits of our labor from the years of sacrifice to obtain the money for this moment. We were going to live in the capital of our province in our own country in our own house at last!

What a tremendous shock we experienced when we opened the door and saw the disaster that another family member had dumped on us. History repeated itself and our "dear" relatives took advantage of us once again.

According to the neighbors there were parties in our house until all hours of the night. The music, the noise, the traffic were unconscionable. The son and his friends danced in the upper patio and bedroom and left empty bottles, used condoms, and food wrappers in every corner. They used the space under the staircase as a second bathroom. Understandably my wife broke into tears and I sank down beside her in a stupor of disbelief. The next day we got up and dug in, literally, with extensive cleaning. Little by little we got the house in order, but it took a whole week just to purge the filth.

Several years later in a moment of weakness we allowed another set of relatives to use a piece of land that we had purchased to plant some fruit trees and to cultivate some vegetables. It was near the airport in La Laguna and in the heat of the summer it was a great place for picnics because it was up in the cooler valley away from the coast. These cousins roasted whole pigs and strew the bones, the paper products, the soda cans, and the wine bottles all about the property. They picked our fruit and vegetables when we were not there, yet never trimmed, nor watered, nor hoed as a gesture of thank you. It got so bad that the neighbors complained about the smell of the accumulated garbage. Once again we had to clean up what was ours after others; selfish others who had no concept of consideration nor gratitude.

With the amassing of all of these unthinkable dastardly deeds directed toward us, I ultimately approved of my son's stand regarding his extended family. He proclaimed publicly and vociferously that he had no family in the Canary Islands except for his parents. As I stated earlier in this book my wife was the oldest of eight and I was the third of also eight. So there were a passel of aunts, uncles, nieces, nephews, and cousins, and not a one who sided with us on any matter. They were either outwardly antagonistic, sneaky, or indifferent. I can only assume that their outrageous behavior was dictated by the teachings of the two despotic patriarchs, Eleuterio Barbuzano and Marcelino González. They instilled in their children that both Saturnino, me, and Guadalupe, my wife, and consequently Enrique, my son, were not part of their family and childhood memories are hard to overcome.

With hindsight I now feel that my son was lucky to discover such treachery at such a young age. It gave him strength to endure, to resist, and to escape. The best thing that he did was not to follow my wishes and come to live in the Canary Islands especially in El Hierro. He doesn't have to live among non-friends, nor pseudo-family members. He doesn't have to see them, nor listen to them, nor tolerate them, but I do.

Hypocrisy can be a necessary tool for survival when you're functioning among dormant enemies who pretend to be your friends. These self-centered individuals in their goal to attain whatever they want, however they want, are relentless. They are like dripping water that droplet by droplet weakens the foundation of your very soul.

I should not have paid any attention to what they said especially when they predicted my son's future. The all-seeing gossips turned out to be totally wrong about him. As a child they called him a savage like Tarzan of movie fame, because he liked to roam the forest and the mountain slopes communing with nature. As a man they referred to him as crazy, when they saw him jogging for health, while their cohorts drank to excess.

They called him irresponsible, because he lived in America and not close by to his parents. Yet he came all the way from The United States twice a year for over forty years to visit them. Some locals live down the street from the mother and father and rarely stop by. The comments even continued when we ended up in the nursing home. They said that our children would dump us there and abandon us. Never happened; the visits were constant. According to the staff, many of their residents don't receive visitors and the family members are just down the hill,or over a few blocks.

The malcontents bet that my son's marriage would not last more than a year. After all he was marrying a "gringa' and as everyone knows the American woman wears the pants in the family. Again they miscalculated. My son and his first and only wife are heading for 50 years of noticeable marital bliss. The tongue waggers said that the son of a dirt poor farmer from the perimeters socially and topographically of the town would never amount to anything, but today he is way better off than any of them. Envy is all on their side and pride is on mine.

My son was diligent in his efforts to support his wife and child. He was determined to get a university degree to assure their future. The uncle of a friend of his was particularly helpful because he, as an orphan, had to also struggle to get ahead and he became a medical doctor. He encouraged my son in his studies and would give him work on his estate so that he could earn the money to pay for his education.

This doctor was a multi-millionaire with several private clinics yet they became friends. Gilbert said that he saw himself in Enrique and that he appreciated that this friend never took advantage of him because of his wealth. He never felt that his protegé was cultivating the friendship for financial favors and side benefits. One day this man showed up at my son's modest little house and said, "Here are two tickets round trip for your parents to come to Michigan. After all that you have told me about them, I want to meet them."

Guadalupe and I went. It was an opportunity for us to see for ourselves how our son and his family were doing. Also if a rich man expressed a desire to know us, I also looked forward to talking to this generous gentleman. He invited us to his home. He took us out to eat often. He got permission to fly his six-seater airplane over Niagara Falls just for us. Niagara Falls is the largest waterfalls in the world in terms of volume of water cascading over its rim. The "Salto de Angel" in Venezuela is the tallest. The Iguazú Falls in Argentina is the largest in terms of area. I learned this from my daughter-in-law, the teacher.

The view of Niagara from the air was impressive at least from the glimpses I saw when I ventured to open my eyes. Yet what impressed me most of all from our visit was the man himself. I had never met anyone like him. Here was a rich man who treated me, a poor man, with respect. I had never experienced this reception in Spain. The rich Spaniard wants the poor man to know his inferior place and stay there, so that he can reign from his superior position.

My daughter-in-law's family received us with open arms, and by the way, they were far from poor. They had a lovely big house filled with beautiful antique furniture. The language barrier made communication challenging, but their actions spoke volumes. When I saw my son with his American family, I was very pleased for him. We thought that he was making a mistake marrying outside of his culture. Now after all these years I have concluded that he was truly fortunate in his choice of wife as I had been.

My wife and I really wrestled with fate to win a decent standard of living. My son and his wife also started out with very little and achieved a lot. The typical American helps the children some, but not too much. They need to learn to stand on they own two feet. My son never depended on the inheritance from us as so many Spanish offsprings do. Many young people that I see in Spain, in contrast, believe that they deserve everything: a fancy car, a new computer, brand name clothing, a mobile phone, but they expect it all to be given to them. Let someone else pay, namely the parents.

The grandparents and great-grandparents who lived through the pre and post Civil War periods, tried to give their progeny the best of the best, to give them what they never had. Sadly the parents who shower their children with so much often create self-centered brats. They demand things and pay for nothing, neither with money, nor with returned favors. Since they never learn to defend for themselves financially, the distant inheritance becomes their goal, their way of securing a future without working for it.

The concept of inheritance is a very ingrained custom in all of Spain. The children start calculating their share in prepubescent years. They are all counting on it even before the demise of the parents. This situation by its very nature creates conflict. In order to receive the inheritance the parents have to die. Which desire is the greater? How much of a driving force is the need for money?

The parents on the other side of the coin take advantage of the fact that they control the money and the properties meanwhile. Some of them play favorites pitting one brother against another for their affection. A well know phrase captures this idea. You often hear a parent say, " Everything that I have goes to my children. I did it all for them, but its all mine until I die." My son commented about this two way manipulation by paraphrasing a proverb, "A moving van doesn't accompany the funeral procession to the cemetery".

Don't the elders grasp the fact that they can't take it with them?

The very institution described above undermines any family unity. Actually it foments dissension. It causes sibling against sibling to vie for the position of the most favored in the will. Since both sides are hypocritical in showing their true feelings and the game has an undetermined ending, the expressed love is bound to wither away long before the actual passing of the head of the household.

Isn't it almost satirical that those who are waiting for the inheritance are in reality waiting for their parents' death? You can't have one without the other. With Mom and Dad alive all the sons and daughters have is a promise for the future and no benefit in the present.

My wife and I had only one child on purpose. We were both the least favorite of all our siblings. We knew what rejection was and found out at the reading of the wills how true it was. We both had to fight for our fair share.

Now with the wisdom of age I once again thank my son for putting things in perspective. He sought his own fortune and never counted on the inheritance from us. My advice to the modern generation is to motivate their children from a very early age to become self-sufficient, instead of holding the idea of inheritance over their heads. The inheritance could then be a gift rather than an insurance policy and the heirs would no longer be on opposing teams.

When I saw that I couldn't continue to manage my affairs, I entrusted all of my bank accounts and properties to my son. He never touched a penny nor sold any of the properties. He gave me whatever quantity of money I asked for. Occasionally I would request a thousand "euros" (the currency of Europe including Spain) to keep in the nursing home since I was in a wheelchair and couldn't get to the bank whenever I wanted. He advised against it for it could be stolen easily, but he did not refuse to give them to me. He said that it was my money and I could do with it what I wanted.

My son's actions confirmed to me that the best way to establish familial harmony is to help our children help themselves, and to withdraw the dependency of inheriting. Create love, not war!

Chapter 13
Years of Joy, Years of Despair

Ramon's dream house that he built himself

After returning to the mother country it took several years to put our houses in order both in the big island of Tenerife and the small island of El Hierro. We found everything neglected. Those whom we trusted to care for our properties did nothing to maintain them. The reconstruction would take time, but now at least we were home and had the time and dedication to do so.

It was during this period that my son came for a visit with his wife and little son. He was now 26 and he hadn't been back since he was thirteen. His wife told me later that she remembered standing on the deck of the boat next to her husband approaching the tiny port when he faintly mumbled, "I don't know what I feel coming back here; such ambivalent thoughts of the hatred of so many people and of the love of the nature that was my refuge."

He saw that we were doing okay, but he suggested that we diversify our savings by buying some land which is almost always a good investment. He also added that it was not a good idea to have all your money in just one bank. I took in consideration the one piece of advice and tabled the other for later. We found a few acres of land on the highway up to the volcano El Teide on the outskirts of the town at the base. It had a little house for shelter meeting the basic needs and would be ideal for a bit of farming.

This was the onset of the good years. My son was comfortable in The United States and we concurred that it was the moment for us to start enjoying our life to the fullest. We planted fruit trees and some vegetables on the plot. We remodeled the cabin. I built a garage with extra large space for farm tools and for the Renault car that I had bought used since at 50 I had just learned to drive.

We spent our days between the house in the center of the capital near the stores and the beautiful parks and our mini-hacienda in the valley of the surrounding mountains. In the summer we would go to the little island to escape the heat of city life. We were delighted to be able to inhabit the houses that I had constructed myself slowly over the years and with many self denials of material comforts. We relived the memories of the difficult periods with thankful appreciation of what we had achieved together against all odds. How rewarding it was to see the fruit of our labor.

Now that we were no longer seen as a burden to others, friends and family came out of the woodwork. The visits were many and the favors asked for numerous. We were willing to do the favors because we were experiencing relationships that we had not had before. We thought that now we had friends and that the family members' attitude toward us was softening.

These were the years of contentment. For the first time we were functioning without money worries. With this economic independence we didn't need to work. We were receiving some rent from a few of our properties. We had substantial savings in the Santa Ella Bank which paid a higher interest rate than the others. All of the above lent to a very comfortable life style, a life that we never imagined possible for two people who started out their married life sleeping in a borrowed bed in a rented hayloft.

Then disaster struck! On May 9, 1976 the Sunday edition of the local newspaper announced that the Santa Ella Bank had closed its doors and all interest payments were suspended. All accounts were frozen pending further investigation of the disappearance of the vice-president and the missing funds. Chaos exploded. The reverberations brought the injured parties out in hordes. The lines outside the bank went on for blocks. 7000 families were affected including us. Some people who lost everything committed suicide. Some went crazy with grief. I had a heart attack and my wife entered into a depression that lasted over two years. We had lost 90% of our money. If only I had listened to my son's advice to spread the money out over several different banks.

Again we faced the reality that we had no other option than to gather up the pieces and inch forward. My wife took in embroidery work from a local store that catered to the tourists and I planted potatoes to sell. These two endeavors gave us the means to put food on the table and occasionally purchase a needed article of clothing. Thank Heavens we owned all our properties and land outright.

The proportion of our visitors escalated after our terrible loss. Why? Some did come to commiserate. Others came to snoop, but others came to test the waters. How deep was our desperation? They wanted to assess the possibility of obtaining some of our properties dirt cheap. They were like a pack of wolves waiting for the weak to succumb.

My son's godfather materialized out of the blue under the guise of a dear friend to counsel me to sell my Suarez Guerra house in the capital. He said and I paraphrase, "Sell your house. You need the money. Don't try to save it for your son to inherit. That ingrate is never coming back here to live. If you want, I could buy it from you. I couldn't afford much, but as a favor to a friend like you, blah, blah, blah."

We never intended to sell. We would never have given up our hard-earned possessions without a fight. It wasn't really a great surprise to learn several months later that the godfather had a buyer in the wings who had promised him a hefty commission. Again we were dealing with a "friend" whose personal gains outweighed the well being of his "compadre" and godson.

Although my age did not yet qualify me for government retirement benefits, my doctor recommended that I apply. He thought that there was a good possibility with my poor health after the heart attack and my military record. It was approved.

On the day I went to pick up my first check, I met one of my brothers-in-law on the way. I told him of my fortunate luck and his response was. "To tell you the truth I don't envy you, because it was your poor health that got you the benefits. Quite a price to pay, don't you think?" Through the grapevine I heard that he went to apply the very next day for his retirement benefits claiming disabilities that he didn't have. Since these ailments were fictitious his petition was denied. A few days later his wife let her guard down and in anger complained that if I had gotten the government funds, why shouldn't her husband? It wasn't fair, and so on and so on, whine, whine, whine. Their true feeling was of resentment. They didn't want us to be better off than they were.

My son says that I am like the mythical Phoenix. He related how this bird of lore came alive again and rose up from its own ashes. His praise was for the times that I was felled by fate and repeatedly lifted myself up to fly once more. With my retirement income and the produce from the farming we were able to stand again our own two feet. Our finances were secure, but now a series of health problems began and slowly worsened with age. Both my wife and I never really recuperated from the blows suffered. My mind was raring to go, but my body protested and often went on strike.

It was during our dark days that there was an economic boom for the Canary Islands and El Hierro gained the most because it had the least. The European Common Market infused funds to pave roads, install electricity, and to construct buildings such as community centers, sports arenas, and medical clinics. The principal source of construction materials was rock and volcanic rock was the best because it was porous and easy to work with. This rock was utilized in highways, boundary walls, and could be used for decorative facades for governments offices.

When my father-in-law died and his children met to decide on the division of the inheritance, we were far away in Venezuela. Remember that my wife was the invisible sister, the daughter whose name was not allowed to be uttered in her father's house. However, the law would not permit them to erase her from consideration. So the siblings agreed to assign her the worst piece of land, extensive, but worthless. It was rocky terrain where nothing would grow and on a slope that was battered by the winds of the frequent stormy sea.

Can you imagine their consternation when the demand for volcanic rock became primordial in all the construction going on? Probably every time that they saw a loaded truck leave their sister's land, they ground their teeth like the machines that chipped away at the rock in our quarry. Needless to say it produced another not so little income for us.

Eventually we tired of going back and forth between the two islands and decided to live permanently in El Hierro. We relinquished the keys and responsibility to my son who spent time in the capital when he came for vacations. We chose the house on the coast in the town of El Golfo because it had the best climate and the most beautiful view of the ocean. We attended the activities in the senior citizens' club; playing cards, or domino, or bingo. There were birthday parties and holiday festivities. There was always someone to talk to and many of them we had known from childhood. Finally we were looking forward to peace and quiet that all old folks deserve to enjoy.

We were enchanted with our house, the one that I labeled as my master piece among the four that I had built. Behind our site was a semi-circle of steep mountainous terrain, and before us the volcanic cliffs of the ocean with its magnificent waves spray painting white against black. At dusk the illumination of the street lamps snaked serpentine-like from the church at the foot of the eastern cliff through the town and on to the setting sun in the west.

I had planted some fruit trees and vegetables in the little plot behind the house. I had my workshop in my garage where I tinkered with fixing things and creating inventions. As the years passed my energy and capabilities diminished and my repairs went undone. When I no longer could do any favors for friends and relatives, the visits waned and soon there were none. Those who claimed to be my friends didn't feel the need to come to see me anymore.

Then one day a nephew, who I hadn't seen in years, appeared at the door. He was with his mother and his third "wife" (Who knows what to call them these days when they're not married, but are parading around as if they were.) His mother was the infamous sister-in-law who negated food to my son and who pretended to be crazy to avoid the responsibilities of caring for a new-born. My wife and I chose to receive them since the nephew was not at fault for his mother's behavior, and for his sake we went out with them to restaurants. We accompanied them to typical tourist places that they had not seen since the economic boom.

After the fact I realized that we had made a mistake being seen with them in public on so many different occasions. This relative could have been an outstanding military strategist because she planned her campaign with such cunning. People said after she left, "How can it be possible that that woman is as diabolical as the son asserts? They wouldn't have gone all around the island with someone who treated their son so badly". Madame General's strategy worked; she undermined the credibility of her worst critic.

Of course, my son was livid. "I can't conceive of how you and the herreños treat those who abuse you as if nothing had ever happened." In retrospect the nephew talked about his wealth and his future plans which my son never believed. At the time of the writing of these memoirs we haven't seen him again nor any signs of his grandiose plans in motion.

I made another error in taking them to my son's house which was the same house where they had spent so much time before immigrating to Venezuela. They made no comment whatsoever on the remodeling or the modern conveniences added. Envy prevented them from saying anything positive regarding my son.

When they were in our house, they couldn't avoid seeing the pictures of Enrique and his family and again not a word. Out of courtesy they should at least have asked. "How's your son?" and moved on to other topics. It was as if my son didn't exist. I was receiving the infamous mother politely in my home out of respect for her son's feelings. They should have mentioned my son in passing, however briefly, out of consideration for my wife and me.

The system of using someone to wound another is a common practice in the island. My son had always hated hypocrisy and refused to play the game. He wouldn't keep quiet at an act of injustice, nor tolerate manipulation. Therefore, the manipulators tried to get to him through us or vice versa. Sometimes they would try to blame us for something that my son did or said. I would respond by setting the record straight, "My son is my son and he is entitled to his opinions. Why don't you ask me for my thoughts on the matter"?

Here's an example of what I mean. One of my brothers-in-law came to the nursing home for the first time after we had been there over a year. My wife, his sister, was bedridden dying of cancer. In his audacity he blamed my son's behavior for the reason that he had not visited in a long time. In anger I retorted, "Yes, my son stated publicly that he has no family here in the island and with reason for their behavior toward him from childhood. But my wife and I never said that, nor have we ever done anything or said anything against you, no matter how tempting."

The only link between you and me is that shadow of a woman over there who you have treated so badly repeatedly, and you have the guts to come and complain about others. You came to excuse your behavior and shift the blame, but you never once looked at your sister, nor took her hand in sympathy. Now with the pending loss of the love of my life, you are no longer anything to me. You may leave, you are no longer needed here." My son would have been proud of me. I finally sent my nemesis to hell.

As you know my son had the luxury to speak his mind because he didn't live here among these people. My wife and I had to endure in silence because the consequences were lurking just outside the front door. If you are on the tennis court, you can't refuse to play the game and not return the serve. You'll take a beating by a barrage of balls being aimed at your face.

I have understood for quite a few years why my son held such strong anti-herreño sentiments. He suffered as a child their rejection and as an adolescent he bore the unjust punishments generated by their false accusations. We, however, chose to return to our roots no matter how rotten, because they were what we knew and what we were comfortable with. We had hidden knowledge of our trials and tribulations from him so one, he would not worry about us long distance; two, his anger wouldn't consume him; and perhaps three, we didn't want to admit to the reality of some of his observations regarding the nature of the herreños.

It has taken me a long time to do the numbers and put two and two together, but now in my nineties I bow down to the champion of lost causes, my son, Enrique Barbuzano González. He was right about the family not caring, about most of the herreños being selfish and manipulative, and about me being, in part, responsible for some of my own problems. I let some people take advantage of me due to my ignorance or necessity, but I was also guilty of buying the illusion of the paradise that the inhabitants like to present to the outside world. To paint a pretty picture makes the reality in which we have to live a little more palatable. I convinced myself that my acquaintances had changed and they swore that they had. But it is impossible to change others, perhaps one of the major reason for so many failed marriages today. You can only change yourself, but it takes a long, long time. It only took me 95 years.

Chapter 14
Shedding of the Lies

All things come to an end

In my island silence and hypocrisy move along side by side. The carriers of these diseases play dominos together. They eat at the same table in parties and restaurants. They cover for one another's misdeeds, no matter how treacherous. The motivation for the behavior is always the same, either fear, or benefit.

The fear that I refer to is not physical since it rarely occurs. There are few conflicts that are resolved face to face. The vast majority of vengeful actions are done in anonymity, behind the back, under the cover of darkness, or by means of a third party.

Your silent enemies disguise themselves as outspoken friends. They show outrage at the destruction of your crops which they instigated. They lament the robbing of your possessions that they surreptitiously committed. The hungry may slaughter your animals to fill their stomachs, but the malicious ones kill to inflict pain on the man that they have chosen to hate for reasons known only to them. Over a span of about thirty years six of my dogs and cats have been poisoned. They have paid the ultimate price for having been the recipients of my affection and the tool of my enemies' revenge.

These secret avengers, when they're in their hypocritical mode, talk of principles such as honor, integrity, respect. The individual who is the most lacking in these values is the one most adamant in their defense. Of course, many credulous people will believe that he is the upstanding citizen that he purports to be. An example, one of my many nephews once said and I quote, "Well, I don't rob from my friends". How principled he thought he was!

The man or woman who suffers from these deceitful acts will know, or at least suspect, who the guilty party is. Yet he maintains silence and pretends in a reciprocal hypocritical way that he has no idea. When he encounters by chance the culprit, he stops and has a drink with him so that he will not detect any change in behavior. He knows that if he doesn't keep quiet, they'll continue stealing and killing his livestock and pets. Thus the game goes on without end and without winners.

Something you learn early in life is not to make comments about your suspicions, nor to ask too many questions. You could be talking to a villager who claims that he knows nothing, when he knows everything. He could be protecting himself from being labeled an informer or just hiding his own culpability. It could very well be that the man drinking coffee with you is a good friend of the man you consider guilty of the travesty against you. They might even have committed the crime together.

In a small town the people know everything yet publicly negate knowing anything. If the information could affect them adversely, they keep quiet; if it doesn't, ooh delectable gossip. Sometimes they may even whisper the name of the person responsible for the wicked deed. Then they add, "but I'll deny that I told you anything and if you go to court, there is no way that I will serve as a witness."

I have lived in this atmosphere of intrigue and deceit all of my life, and I too kept silent, whispered, and refused to defend. There was no other way to survive and protect the little that you had. I couldn't afford to make any more enemies especially when I didn't even know who most of them were.

Now after all this time and with ninety plus years I have excessive time to ponder, ruminate, review the haunting memories of things well done and things gone sour. One day the thought came to me, "What a high price I have paid for keeping mute. Most of all I have buried the true me and never let him out. My behavior was dictated by others. So little by little I tore away the layers and allowed myself to emerge. This, my final book, is my debut.

It took me a long, long time to realize that I was hollow inside; the real me was missing. I am so tired of manipulations. I encounter so many lies and find in me so little patience. Often when I'm seated at my typewriter I desire to go backward, not forward. I reminisce of the old days as I guess many oldsters do.

I remember the green fields in the spring and the smell of the harvest; the cutting of the grapes on the coast and the reaping of the wheat on the high plateau. I can recall the farmers at dawn going out to their land with their beasts of burden. Some would be talking as they walked along in groups. Others, if they were plodding along alone, might be singing. I can envision the old houses with their roofs of straw, the dirt roads with the clouds of dust kicked up by the passing feet, and the maze of black volcanic walls marking the boundaries where one should not go. All of this was perched on top of the mountain with spectacular views.

There was a certain peacefulness that reigned over the countryside which tamped down the aura of the poverty of the times. This aspect of my island has always charmed me and this is perhaps in part what led me back to the place where I was so mistreated. It is sometimes the land and not the people that calls to your heart.

I am at an age with hours to spend on nothing. I will be here tomorrow, and the day after, and next week without anything really to do but think. We old folks are very much aware that the end is near, but of course we don't know when. So you confront and rejoice with each new day as it comes.

We don't want to cause trouble or be ignored. We don't want to lose the little bit of help so desperately needed that a few people give us. Because of the limited physical and sometimes mental capabilities due to advanced years, we can no longer function alone or defend ourselves. We rely on others and even though their attention of caring may be false, it is preferable to distain and indifference.

Some people think that they can fool me and they don't realize their error. I know that the majority of individuals who stop by my house, don't do it because they care. Do they come to see how we are feeling, to help us, or to ask if we need anything? No!

Some come to sell a service and others just to see for themselves our predicament. They enjoy finding something negative which gives them fodder for the ever turning gossip mill. As our need for assistance augmented the visits diminished. The few who did come stayed briefly and returned sporadically.

Our good friends in the town, who had greeted and received us so warmly, pass in front of the house and do not enter. Our buddies from the senior citizens, with whom I had regularly played cards and my wife had chatted with, don't appear.

I tried to find a reason not to feel this way, but I couldn't talk myself out of it. The biggest dilemma that old folks have is disillusionment. We are isolated by family and friends. We have no one to converse with. The younger ones, even just by a decade or so, make us sense that we are forgotten, useless, no longer of service to anyone. Just throw away the old furniture and make room for the new.

For the "ancient ones" the truth of yesterday is the lie of today. They say that we complain without cause. We don't comprehend clearly how much money we have. We don't know what we're talking about half the time. This ruse of senility is the weapon used to rob and abuse the elderly.

They take our money. They destroy our dignity. They pass judgment on our credibility when we try to protect what's ours. We haven't died yet, we have just been made invisible. We are simply shadows of the past that are slowly fading away, but not fast enough for some.

My wife and I are considering going into assisted living. Alone in the house or alone in the "old folks home", what difference does it make? Our situation is getting more and more tedious. I can hardly walk and my wife keeps forgetting things like turning off the stove. In the "residencia", as it is called here, my wife would not have to cook, nor clean, nor wash clothes. I could get help with my limited mobility. We both could be aided to monitor our medications.

In the home there would be people to talk to and the personnel would attend to us decently. Even though they are paid to do so, we would still benefit. I will be able to use my "free" time to work on my book. I asked my son to finish it after my death using my copious notes. My son and I selected together the title "El Precio del Silencio" which translates as *The Price of Silence.**

When my wife and I cease to exist, that will be the moment to break through the walls of silence with my book and finally tell the truth about our life. It will be the time to demand payment for my silence. I want this book to be my voice from the graveyard and I will at last be free of the chains that had held me prisoner for so long.

If someone should be offended by what is expressed here in these pages and wants to question my comments, you know where you can find me. Please forgive me, if I don't pay too much attention. Been there, did that. It's over.

**Translator's note: The title in English was converted into "The Burden of Silence" instead of "The Price of Silence" because it was felt that it better captured the nuance of the "cross to bear" rather than death as a penalty.*

Chapter 15
Peace and Disappointment

77 years of marriage

La Residencia de los Ancianos, as assisted living is referred to here in the Canary Islands, became our home more out of resignation than anything else. We resisted like so many others of our age, but as it turned out it was the best decision that we could have made in light of our circumstances.

Let's look at the facility in a neutral way and set aside all the negative horror stories perpetuated by those who want to hold onto their possessions by any means including blackmail. "If you don't take care of me in my own house, I won't give you your share of the inheritance."

The building is located in El Valle de El Golfo. Eons ago the volcano exploded sideways and the sea rushed in. Several towns were established along this volcanic shelf with the crashing waves below and above the imposing mountain side in the shape of a horseshoe. This cradle of nature forms one of the most picturesque views on the island and the one that we enjoy from the veranda of the "residencia".

This zone called Frontera is not home to the capital, but it has a better climate. Many stores, banks, office buildings, and a cultural center offer the services needed. There are three structures that are clearly visible to the visitor as he comes around the curve of the old two lane highway: the church, the cemetery, and the nursing home. The church is unique because of the separate bell tower. It stands alone, as if on sentinel duty, on a miniature volcanic vent a ways from the sanctuary itself.

The cemetery, although it lies on the outskirts of town, shines in the sun with its white walls contrasting with the soft green of the bushes and plants on the slopes at its base. The mountain with its dusty desert colors seem to set a beautiful yet somber backdrop. People rarely think about it or enter in. Those who will go there someday rather not be constantly reminded. The neglected cats have found a haven among the departed who can no longer do them harm.

In between the church and the cemetery the building of the "tercera edad" is really quite pretty. "Tercera edad" is a term used to describe those in the third stage of their lives: child, adult, senior. In English a nice phrase is "their golden years". The edifice is two stories high and the site slightly elevated so that the view of the town, the sea, and the mountain are all part of our daily scope. It has a wide and elongated terrace with flowers planted here and there. At the bottom of the driveway there is a clinic with visiting doctors and nurses.

There is an elegance and tranquility about the location and the distance keeps the noise at bay. Even though it is in walking distance from the main street and the local farmers' market, many never come up the hill. They say that it is too depressing to encounter their dear so-called loved ones or cherished friends in a nursing home. How much more depressing it is for those of us within these confines, knowing that our long time acquaintances are just down the hill and can't be bothered to come up.

For those of us in the "residencia" the church and cemetery go unnoticed. We know that they exist, but there's no need to mention them. Very few at our age want to discuss religion. We either are believers or not. It's not a time to change. And why talk about the cemetery? It's just another thing that is not going to be altered.

Now commenting about the nursing home is a horse of a different color. Everyone has something to say and it's usually negative. The residents know who has just arrived, who was taken out, and who has died. They especially relish the topic of the reasons that brought the newcomer to their lair.

In their way of thinking there are only two reasons that a person comes to this facility. One reason is that they did not have the money to pay for someone to take care of them in their own home. The other cause of internment is that the heirs want to enjoy the inheritance now, to live in what they consider their house, to plant or sell their land according to their criteria, not the old man's.

Regardless of the impetus that brings them the vast majority do not enter these walls voluntarily. I believe that many senior citizens themselves spread the rumors of horrible conditions in the "residencia" with the purpose of making their children feel guilty about sending them here. If the sons and daughters don't accept the burden of their care out of love, it seems that the parents want to shame them into doing it.

It shouldn't come as a surprise that I was one of those guys who listened to the negative press; how they drugged the old folks to control them, how they made you take a cold shower in the middle of the night, how the food was leftovers from the restaurants.

My son said that he wouldn't force us to go into the nursing home. So he and I looked into what he calls the "mujer mágica". This is a woman according to my cohorts who can be hired to care for you at home. My son gave them this nickname because this figure exists only in the minds of the wishful. If they do it for money, service falls a little short. If they attend the elderly with the hopes of being generously remembered in the will, then they wouldn't desire for them to have a long and healthy life, would they?

We tried several times to find such a woman, but each case was disastrous. We were wiling to pay a salary and in addition give her and her family one of our houses to live in rent free so that they would be nearby in case of emergencies.

My wife discovered the first one leaving the house with some small pictures off the wall, some new dish towels and a tablecloth, plus some toys that had been our grandson's all tucked into her tote bag. The bulky bag caught her attention, because the "helper" had arrived with it practically empty. I guess she felt helper meant "help yourself." Another one was amenable to the plan, but she wanted to remodel our offered house to her liking, "Let's knock down this wall, and replace…"

Whenever they saw that they could not get their way, or that the work constituted more than they thought that it would be, they quit, they didn't show up, or they walked away in a huff. Three times my son encountered problems on his visits regarding home care personalities. The "mujeres mágicas" were not enchanting and they dissipated like smoke, leaving no trace of their agreed upon services.

The last attempt at this solution was the worst. It was a young couple expecting a baby and they gushed about how they wished that their parents were more like "don" Ramón and "doña" Guadalupe. "Let me shave you and cut your toenails. Let me help you to wash the dishes and launder the clothes." They couldn't do enough until they broached the subject of the house. "If you would sign this document bequeathing us one of your houses, we will attend to your every need." I answered, "I can't do that, everything is in my son's name." And that was the day of the great metamorphosis. They threw down our medicines on the table and left for the island of Lanzarote for a two week vacation, leaving us in limbo between Heaven and Hell; Heaven recent assistance, Hell current abandonment.

When my son returned to the island they had also returned and after almost a physical confrontation with the probable non-husband, my son had to get a court order to evict them. They moved out in the middle of the night taking everything that was not nailed down even the simple things like the brooms and dustpans.

The next time that my son traveled to the islands he received a call to come and get me even before he had time to unpack. I was bleeding profusely and had driven myself to the local clinic. They said that I needed to go to the hospital in the capital twenty minutes away, but refused to summons an ambulance. My son had to transport me in his car.

After losing his temper and the argument over the ambulance, they informed him in the hospital without waiting for test results that I had prostate cancer. It turned out not to be true, but we all lived for a week or more with the agony that so many cancer patients must have to face. At that moment I knew from these events that I would have to go to the assisted living for my sake, my wife's, and my son's.

Without family and friends we would be at the mercy of people who controlled the rights to ambulances and yielded the power to pronounce your possible imminent death. There would be those who could not pass up the opportunity of tricking an old couple who were alone and unable to defend themselves. The fear of such subjugation would be psychologically debilitating. Let the nursing home arrange for these things, I thought at last. Mismanagement of care would be too obvious coming from the government facility.

We reluctantly began to prepare ourselves for the move to the home. We concurred that we would get the help that we required and that there would be other people to talk to like having a constant supply of visitors. I told my wife that I with my crutches could get assistance in bathing and getting dressed. She who was always thinking of others added, "And I won't be a burden to anyone. I'll make my bed, help set the tables, and sweep the halls. I like to sweep."

With trepidation we braced ourselves for the inevitable not knowing exactly what to expect. My son and daughter-in-law assured us that they would continue to come to visit a couple of times a year. And they kept their word.

Once established we met all kinds of people. Some were content, insolent, joking, resigned, or embittered. It all depended on their basic character and the manner of their arrival. My wife and I adapted as we had had to do so many times in our lifetime. We made the best of it and moved on.

The feuds from outside came clinging to their participants like the ever present fleas of the old days. The infestation of their hatred made them critical of each other and they would refuse to sit next to an enemy of past ages. Others, who were disillusioned with their children for having interned them here, sat in silence daring anyone to cross over into their field of misery and mistrust.

Others accepted their situation philosophically and with a sense of humor. It was with these few that my wife and I spent our time. We shared the stories of the old days and tried not to think too much about the future. There was one man in particular that I was glad to have met for his sake and mine. He had reached such a profound depth of depression that he considered taking his own life.

This man had been very popular in the political scene and very active in the folkloric groups. It was a great change for him to come to the assisted living out of necessity due to an increasing lack of mobility like me. He suffered an even bigger shock when his family and friends drifted away removing with them his feeling of importance. He said that the friendship that developed between him and us saved his life. I am humbled to consider that and I also am grateful to him for making our stay so much more entertaining.

The "residencias" in Spain are a godsend to the inhabitants in their golden years where families are distant by geography or choice. Immigration separated many families after the Spanish Civl War. Unfortunately the administration of these facilities is dictated by political trends. The director is selected by the winning party as a favor for his or her support. It doesn't matter if they are qualified or not.

A few weeks after our arrival the director was replaced by a very young woman fresh out of law school who had lost in her attempt to be elected to a political post. She tried her best to do a good job. Her persistence, dedication, and affection for her own grandmother aided her in attaining a level of comfort and confidence in her new duties.

Even though she came to us as a pawn of the political system, she accomplished a lot during her tenure. Taking care of "grumpy" old men and women is not easy and I grew to have great respect and admiration for her and for the personnel under her command. We enjoyed each other's company and spent many hours conversing on the terrace.

After only a year in this situation my wife became ill and they diagnosed her with colon cancer. The socialized medical system delayed months before sending her to the bigger island of Tenerife and it was probably too late. After her operation the doctors said that they were unable to eradicate the cancer and that she had at best less than a year to live.

Prior to the operation she had signed a document when she converted to be a Jehovah Witness denying any blood transfusions. My son had just arrived from The States and when he went to the hospital to see her, the Jehovah Witnesses were there claiming to be her representatives. My son confronted them and revoked the document by legal means. She had her transfusions and one more year with us. She was so indoctrinated by these religious colleagues that she couldn't bear the thought of displeasing them. When recuperating she rejoiced by expressing her relief, "Wasn't I lucky that I didn't need any transfusions"? For her peace of mind, she had repressed the fact that she did.

When the hospital determined that it was time for her to be sent back to the small island, they notified my son to come and take her in a taxi to the airport. There was to be no ambulance, nor any trained staff to aid in the transport of a very sick, frail, elderly woman home to her anxiously waiting husband.

My son once again had to rear up and fight off the dragons of righteousness breathing fire and obstructiveness. My wife became nervous and started to vomit up blood. So they took her back with an "oops" into their caring embrace. About a week later we were able to bring her home by ambulance, thanks to a friend of my son's who knew people in the political realm of the hospital system.

Due to the arguments with incompetents that my son had to endure on his "vacation" he in turn became ill. A series of sores erupted on his torso and legs, possibly stressed induced. The local medics treated them as infected pimples which they squeezed and drained every day for a week. The low grade fever and throbbing continued for almost a month more. The day after getting back to The United States he went to the dermatologist. Two days later he felt fine and was cured completely by the end of the week. They weren't pimples. They were from a bacterial infection maybe from the water source. No wonder my son does not have much faith in many doctors, especially when they act like gods of medicine and mankind.

When my children came again to the island Guadalupe was gravely ill. She just lay in bed gently moaning nestled up against her friend morphine. They visited each day morning and afternoon for a month or more and then it was time for the final farewell. My son always hated goodbyes so his habit was to pretend that he was coming back the following day.

He stroked his mother's hair and asked her how she felt. "Like a queen", she whispered. He responded as usual, "We'll see you tomorrow." I had sat with my wife awhile with her hands in mine when she opened her eyes a little and inquired in a weakened voice, "Did Enrique leave the island" I said yes and with ever so slight a smile she closed her eyes to rest and so did I. When I awoke with a start I realized that her hand was limp and cold in mine. She had died and at that moment my son was flying across the Atlantic unaware of the sad news that would be waiting for him

The next time that he telephoned and asked how I was doing I lied and replied okay. But the loneliness is intense. I think of my wife constantly. She was everything to me for 77 years of marriage. Since we had no family to rely on she was all my kinships and best friend rolled into one. So I lost more than a wife and other people truly can not imagine the depth of my sorrow.

I pray for the final visit of my old friend, Lady Death. She stopped my wife's suffering and now I long for her to do the same for me. Life is the problem; death is the solution. I wanted to see my son and his wife one more time and Death was a lady. She allowed me to celebrate my 98th birthday with them. My daughter-in-law made a cake and we had a little party in the "old folks home" with my son's friends and a few new ones that I had made.

Both my son and I had the feeling that we would not see each other again. I accompanied them to the terrace as usual and watched as they faded away down the hill each of us raising a hand in a silent salute.

It seemed reminiscent of my departure on the night of the escape by sailboat; the raised arms of goodbye with backs turned silhouetted against the darkening skies. My death is imminent and my leaving my family a certainty, but this time I have no regrets. I hope that my son feels the same way.

A week later the director informed me that they had called for an ambulance to take me to the hospital. I asked my young friend to be sure that my cabinet with the old typewriter and my notes reached my son, and that my electric wheelchair went to the man who defied death to be my friend.

I had already explained to my son that the key to the cabinet was hidden among the keys of the typewriter and that in addition to my notes for this book he would find a wad of bills amounting to about 2000 euros stashed in a secret compartment that I had installed myself.

I know in my heart that I will not return to the "residencia". I will not see the staff members who gave us so much of their time and attention. Thank you, once again for making our final years comfortable and pleasant.

*** *Editor's note: Ramón Barbuzano Morales died a month after celebrating his 98th birthday. He expired in the hospital while asleep as he had hoped, sadly though on his only grandson's birthday, July 14th. Once more his son would receive the news of a loved one's passing from far away.*

The director of the "residencia" assumed her position soon after Ramón and Guadalupe arrived and with the new elections she would be replaced soon after he died. Unwittingly she gave him a one sentence eulogy by saying, "Don Ramón left deep imprints of his having been here within these walls".

It seems as if both Ramón and Guadalupe refused to give into death until their son was safely home in America. One would think that maybe they wanted to save him the pain of the funerals, but it was more. They didn't want him to have to suffer, on top of the obvious, the hypocritical mourning of long absent friends and distant relinquished kinships. Although still living they had died a long time ago. A few hours of feigned respect would not eradicate decades of indifference.

Way before the the assisted living, before the death of the patriarchs, and before the Spanish Civil War two young souls dreamed of a love that they would share for a lifetime. They would struggle together against all odds to achieve these dreams and fulfill the promise until death do us part.

This book is historical, biographical, and philosophical, but most of all it is a love story. It does not end with their demise because they lie along side each other in the cemetery of the town where it all began, united behind two poems appearing on their tombstones which were written by Ramón in honor of his wife.

PART TWO
REFLECTIONS

Chapter 16
The Truth Will Set You Free

Two different worlds; the boy and the man

This is my father's book not mine. He wrote it in his waning years and made me promise to get it published after his death. In it he speaks of the island of El Hierro, the Spanish Civil War, his forbidden marriage, and the abandonment and cruelty by supposed friends and family. I am only the tool he chose to fulfill his dying wish; to tell the truth of his behalf.

I was born in the world that he describes, a world in which I saw and felt as a small child the same cruelty, hatred, and resentment that he had experienced. It was a hostile environment for all three of us. The effects were both physical and emotional, but I think that I overcame them with time, a lot of time. My mother never did. She was scarred for life suffering from a complex of "What did I do wrong?" My father was admirable in that he learned to cope and play the game, yet underneath it all I had the impression that he was always trying to prove himself to those who continually judged him harshly.

When I married in my twenties, I had long talks with my father-in-law who had his university degree in psychology. Dr. Powell helped me to understand why I am the way I am. Thanks to his knowledge and advice I was able to break away from the suffocating bonds of my origins.

He continued to say that the values of my parents, that of honesty, integrity, and self-determination, also had a great influence on me. These beliefs didn't permit me to allow violence to rule my life. He added that my strong character was my salvation. So many negative experiences made me into a fighter. Like the pirates of old I was always prepared to confront anyone with a dagger in my mouth. Out of bad sometimes comes good and at a very early age I decided that I would never be like most of the people from the island of El Hierro. So I tried to be honorable and opposite to the herreños in every way.

The decision to leave home was not just a simple adventure for you continued my father-in-law. It was your way of escaping and searching for freedom, to get as far away as possible, to be able to start anew. The United States gave you many opportunities and you grabbed them. You made of your life what you aspired to, not what those of your childhood pressed upon you. You built your own future brick by brick and you should be very proud of what you have accomplished.

Dr. Powell was right. My feelings from the past have accompanied me to the present. I still don't want to go back to El Hierro, nor the Canary Islands, not even Spain. I can't imagine what kind of man I would have become if I had returned to my roots as my parents wished. When I think of it I envision a man nothing like me and I don't like him.

As I read over my Dad's notes for this book, I came to the conclusion that my father was not as ignorant as I had thought. He had just been pretending, of hiding things he knew about the people that he lived among. He confessed one time that they had lied to me or kept quiet so as not to fan the flames of hatred that they saw smoldering inside of me. Even though he was one of the most honest men that I have ever known, he didn't dare confront the dishonest men, nor denounce their crimes.

He was aware of the maliciousness that surrounded him, but he maintained silence out of fear of repercussions. It has always been very difficult for me to understand this position. In America if you commit a crime, there are consequences. In El Hierro there are many a miscreant walking the streets, serving no time. In fact there isn't even a jail on the entire island. Just for trivia's sake, there are not any traffic lights either.

As I continued to visit my parents and meet many different people, I gradually was able to perceive their world from their point of view that matched my Dad's. One day I was having a cup of coffee with a local shepherd and he told me the following true story. He was watching over his flock of sheep at night and since it was cold he had hunkered down behind a stone wall and covered himself with his wool cape.

He fell asleep, but about midnight he woke up to voices on the other side of the wall. He didn't stand up because he didn't know who they were or what they were up to. He peeked through a gap between the stones and saw two men capture a big, healthy ram and slaughter him for the meat.

The animal belonged to the godfather of his daughter and he had especially raised it for the celebration of his own daughter's wedding. This event happened the day before the nuptials and the shepherd had been invited. He witnessed them putting the edible parts in their pick up truck and throwing the rest of the evidence into the ravine.

The next day when the godfather couldn't find his ram, he asked his friend if he had seen him. "No, I haven't seen him anywhere," he innocently replied, even though he knew exactly what had occurred and had recognized the perpetrators.

I was so surprised by his attitude that I couldn't help myself and had to inquire, "Tell me, if they had killed a man instead of an animal, what would you have done?" With no hesitation whatsoever he responded, "I wouldn't have said a word either. I don't get involved in these things."

So I asked another question, "Why?" His comment woke me up like the slap across the cheek that you give a person in shock. "Because the thieves are rich. They work for the government and I am only a poor shepherd." When I related this to my Dad he wasn't surprised by the man's behavior. He said that he would have done the same thing.

Then he started to unwind a long string of tales about crimes in the island that have gone "unnoticed". No one is serving time. We poor have no voice, no defense. I now comprehend the underlying fear that my parents lived with and why they worried about me, but would never tell me the reason behind their apprehensions.

Isn't it ironic that the silence of honest men make them unwitting accomplices to the criminals? When in the island of El Hierro there are no consequences, the criminals function with a feeling of impunity. The good people are afraid to speak out against the bad, so the greedy with their political connections reign over the land of "peace and tranquility". This is the slogan with which they have brainwashed the majority of peons. The rich get richer and the poor live the lie out of necessity. My parents were no exception.

Of course there are other options, but they could get you marginated or even killed. He who chooses to defend his family and possessions at all cost and to declaim the injustices that he suffers will be confronting conflicts constantly. Battle after battle and no end to the war because he stands alone. Who is he going to invite to the peace table? Those in power can negate him services; his neighbors will deny him friendship. And like the tree that is battered by the wind and the rain he will eventually topple.

I had a friend since childhood who decided to stand up to those who tried to take from him what was his. He became perhaps the most unpopular man on the island being known as a trouble maker with a violent nature. In one of our conversations as adults I advised him that he needed to be more careful, to try to control his temper, and to make an effort to walk away sometimes. Eurico, (which was my name as a child), "I grasp what you're saying, but if you lived here, you would end up worse than me."

I fear that he was right. My blood boils when I see the underdog being mistreated. Like lava it would overflow and I would bowl over anyone in my path until the explosion abated. In the island there is no middle position, you either fight and defend what is yours, or you bow down to the inevitable of losing it.

Soon after this discussion he argued with one of his antagonists and in anger sped away in his truck. He lost control and was killed. I am not suggesting that his truck had been tampered with, but where no laws are enforced, there are no investigations. No matter the cause of the accident the hostile environment directly or indirectly brought about his death. And as incredible as this might seem his funeral was one of the biggest in island history.

When compiling these stories that I have shared and going over my father's notations once again, I felt as if I were reading a novel about people I didn't know, learning about events that my parents never revealed. My mother had commented one time to my wife while they were watching a TV drama, "Oh, I love soap operas, they're so much like real life." My wife gently laughed and responded, "Oh, Guadalupe, they're just exaggerations for entertainment." After having experienced life in El Hierro for about ten years my wife concluded, "Oh my, I had no idea that Guadalupe was correct in her observations. Her whole life has been one continual soap opera and apparently it's still not over yet."

As I reviewed the comments about the people and events that my parents had to endure, another vision focused in my mind of a movie with strange characters filmed in a distant galaxy beyond my imagination. The figures are distorted and the scenery is fuzzy as can happen with technical difficulties.

Like in a science fiction film an eerie feeling pervades and I sense that some foreign creature is vigilant, waiting for its moment to swallow me up. In my daydream the malevolent cloud encircles me and I can detect a flame licking at my legs, next my torso, and then my heart explodes. I wake up with a start and realize that I was overwhelmed by my parents' nightmare. When I recuperate from this weird dream, the fire of hate is gone, dissipated, disappeared.

The instigators of such cruelty toward my parents no longer merit my distain. I think I now feel more sorry for them (but not quite 100%), for they seem to be caught up in their own web of self destruction. Because they have no conscience (maybe a birth defect), they have no remorse. So why waste any more time on them?

After drinking a cup of coffee I returned to the task of my father's book. I savored the taste of relief from having purged the consuming hatred toward these adversaries who were now distant in time and space. At that moment I was no longer a slave to fruitless emotions, no more loathing, just pity.

In contrast I felt great admiration for the persistence and endurance of my parents for the previously unknown depth and intensity of their trials and tribulations. They had until recently divulged only the tip of the iceberg with a birthing here and there of an heinous act that they expected me to let slip away like a chunk of glacier sliding into the ocean eventually floating away and forgotten.

Sadly these feelings came to me after their deaths because they had kept silent about so much for so long. The truth will set you free! I am now proud of my parents rather than resentful. We had always had our differences; they with the attitude, "What will people say?" and me with my habitual retort, "I don't give a blankety-blank-blank!" They insisted that one could not live my way, criticizing and alienating people. You have to close your eyes to many things to keep friends that you might need especially as you grow older. How sorrowful the day when my father realized that the crop of friendships that he had so carefully cultivated died on the vine and left no trace.

They indulged people with caring attention and I treated them with distain for their hypocrisy. Yet we both ended up in the same boat, with few friends. His were new from the nursing home and mine were split. Two or three friends stood by me for decades because we were of the same mind, honest with one another. I had a few new friends because they judged me by what they saw and not by what they heard.

My parents lived and died where they wanted to be and they attained great heights from their humble beginnings. Inadvertently they gave me a leg up to reach my dreams. They now lie side by side in the cemetery of their native village along with estranged family members and long forgotten friends. There are no more feuds in the silence of the tombstones. Everyone is at last equal, until the living come to visit to decorate or to desecrate.

As a tribute to my mother and father, Ramón and Guadalupe, I would like to mention and thank some special individuals. Several times strangers would introduce themselves and state what an honor it was to have known my parents. They expressed their respect and admiration for them. How inexplicable it is that these men and women and those of Santa Cruz de Tenerife had many good things to say. The only ones who ever spoke badly about them were family members.

At seventy years old my mother became a Jehovah Witness. In this religion they call each other brother and sister, and so it was that my mother finally found a family who respected her and showed her affection. I do not care for their beliefs because I saw my mother change from an intelligent woman with an open mind to a robot who could not take action or give an opinion without consulting with her religious advisor. However, thanks to the "witnesses" she died happy with the conviction that Jehovah would reunite her with the infant daughter she had lost before I was born.

When I asked her how she felt the last time that I saw her, she told me "like a queen." This is the memory that I will cherish of her for the rest of my life; dying yet happy, suffering but not complaining, reassuring me that she was fine and that I was not to worry.

My father confessed that after her death he had loss the will to live. When my wife and I left him on the day of his 98th birthday, my wife said, "Happy birthday and I'm sure you'll make it to 100". As we were returning to the car my wife implored, "What did I say wrong? Why did he look like he was going to cry?" I shared with her his comment that he didn't have the desire to continue living.

This is the man who loved his island where his life began, the man who wrote three books praising its natural beauty. I was fortunate to have been present at one of the ceremonies introducing his most recent publication. Among the dignitaries were the Mayor of the island government and the Minister of Culture. To the diversity of people attending from different social and economic backgrounds The Minister of Culture referred to my father as a "national treasure" from whom we could all learn a lot about the history of the island.

About five years afterward he died. He was buried within 24 hours as the law required and I couldn't arrive on time. However, my friends informed me that very few people were present at the wake and internment. It didn't surprise me really. After three years in assisted living from 96 years of age to 98 he was no longer of any benefit to the politicians. His friends, who didn't have the time to visit him while alive, chose not to come for the final farewell. They would never see him again, so why bother? I was told that even some family members spoke badly about the deceased loudly enough for others to hear. Is there no rest for the weary?

I searched the internet just to see if there were a mention of the passing of the "national treasure". The honorable, hard working man who loved his El Hierro so, the writer and the poet of humble origins, he who in time gone by had been praised for his efforts, died alone and forgotten without glory, without sorrow. However, in the village where their love was born are two tombstones with inscribed poems honoring their life together. No one was able to undermine their love. It is not buried, but lives on though these his printed words in stone.

With the death of my parents and the publication of this book my father is able to speak out for the first time. Knowing the truth will be told set him free, and fortunately he also set me free. I have no ties any more to the island that had held me back for so many years and I also can say a final farewell.

I am no longer the fish swimming against the current. I am the albatross flying above the waves in the clear morning sky in search of peace on distant shores. There are times, like my Dad had commented, that I think of the past. In spite of all the maliciousness that surrounded me as a child, I remember moments of happiness. I can see myself as a little boy with short pants and barefoot climbing walls and looking for birds' nests. I run after bumble bees and reach out to the butterflies rising up from the wildflowers along the dirt roads. My dog, Perruco, leaps and barks and enjoys it as much as I do.

In my vivid imagination I can conjure up the child that I once was whenever I want to travel back in time. I do not feel loneliness, just the opposite. I blend in complete harmony with nature. With no humans in sight I have the sensation of absolute freedom. In the heart of the man resides the spirit of the little boy. He has always been with me through the years. We have been inseparable.

I am the product of a love between two people that blossomed in a barren field of hate and desperation, but thanks to the determination of my parents and my sense of independence, I am who I am. I am the combination of the memory of the past, the reflection of the present, and the expectation of the future. I am everything that I wanted to be, yet I am wise enough to know that I am nothing in the great scheme of things. I am like the last breath of the dear one who defies death holding on as long as he can. I am the echo of my own voice and I revel in its repetitions, because I am who I am.

Chapter 17
Truth and Pain Go Hand in Hand

The author, the editor, the heir

My father was a very complicated man with great qualities and numerous defects. In the process of organizing his notes for this book and as all the memories good and bad rattled around and knocked me about, I felt the necessity of adding this addendum.

It hit me that I had not had a father until I was almost seventy years old. As a child I was afraid of him for the beatings that he gave me. As a teenager I felt deep resentment for the injustice of his punishments. As a young man I left home to escape from one more herreño who was my Dad.

It is difficult and emotionally draining to recognize these feelings toward my father. Ironically he had qualities in common with his own father. They were both autocratic and were ruled by the adage "Aquí mando yo", which roughly translates as "What I say goes. You have no word in the matter. Don't question my authority."

My father was a great manipulator as were and are many in his native island. The trick is to tell people what they want to hear so that they will do what is beneficial to you. An example, my father built with his own hands a house for me in the small island of El Hierro. He bought a house in the capital of the big island of Tenerife with a little store included so that I could run a business out of the home.

I had told him a million times that I would never return to live in the Canary Islands, but he kept on hoping that his only son would come back and he set up ways to entice me there. It always bothered me when parents claimed that they did such and such a thing for their children, when in reality they were thinking of themselves. As it has turned out all that my parents did in terms of my inheritance has created many headaches, but I am still grateful.

I once overheard my mother say to my father, "I don't think that our son really appreciates his inheritance and all that we have done to attain these things on his behalf." I intervened and responded, "Yes, Mother, I do, especially after learning more and more about the events of your lives that I never knew of before. You both are incredible for what you have achieved."

In fact my parents should be in the "Guiness Book of World Records" or "Ripley's Believe It or Not". HEADLINE: "Young couple emerged from the depths of the Mariana Trench and they reached at almost a 100 years of age the top of Mt. Everest in terms of the magnitude of their accomplishments." It's unbelievable the skills that my parents learned through self perseverance. With no formal training my Dad mastered the arts of building houses, repairing the unfixable, and saving money by becoming his own expert. My Mom honed her talents in the realm of cooking by inventing recipes, sewing by combining scraps to make whole outfits, and administering their meager earnings wisely.

Even though my inheritance has caused me some problems dealing long distance with the Spanish bureaucracy from The States, it has also afforded me with many, many benefits. My parents gave me two of their houses, one in the capital and one in the country. I was able to enjoy them for a couple of decades when my wife and I came for our yearly visits. We could be comfortable in our own homes during our stay.

All of their five houses have provided me with such pleasant reminders of them now that they are gone. I can see signs of their ingenuity in every nook and granny, and the uniqueness often makes me smile in remembrance. As my Dad said in his part of this book the inheritance should be a gift and not an insurance policy. Thanks, Mom and Dad, for the treasure trove of rich memories.

The author of this book is herreño through and through. He was born, he lived, and he expired in his beloved island. In Venezuela he never really adapted and he functioned within the protective confines of the Canary Island colony. He had had many options to select from if he had decided not to go back, but the familiar ways repeatedly called to him like the comfortable chair with the indents all in the right places.

It would be absurd for me to set him aside from the rest of the herreños just because he was my father. We were like two parallel lines going in the same direction but never intersecting. As my world expanded the distance between these two symbolic lines increased and our differences exponentially grew. If we had not been father and son, each of us would have been criticizing the other mercilessly.

The last time that he visited me in The United States he was about 50 years old. In the airport he said goodbye with these words, "If you want to see me again, you'll have to come to the Canary Islands. I'm too old to make these long trips." When he died at 98, I was 73 and I had been making said trip twice a year for over for 40 years. Whether we saw each other was placed into my hands with a little guilt trip thrown in.

Why did my wife and I travel so far so often to visit them? Because they were my parents, because as a person and a son I could not abandon them as their families had done. And because they had endured so much in their lifetime, that they deserved a little peace of mind and to be worry free.

One day when they were still living in their house, but in bad shape physically, I broached the subject of the possibility of them moving into the nursing home. A resounding NO exploded from his lips citing all the rumors that he had heard of the abusive institution. "Why don't you just send me directly to the cemetery?", he mumbled under his breath. He seemed to calm down when I said that I would never force him to go to the assisted living facility. Then I added, "but together we have to come up with a solution."

"Dad, I can't stay here indefinitely, and you two certainly can't remain in the house by yourselves without some kind of support." Not realizing it at the time I threw in the clincher, "What would happen to mother if you were to end up in the hospital or worse, even die before she did?"

When I phoned from America a couple of weeks later, he informed me that he had applied for a place in the "residencia". Having discussed our problem, his and mine, which was their health and subsequent care, we were able to reach an agreement as a family and accordingly a new stage in our relationship as father and son began. The conflicts had been converted to cooperation and we attained the precious commodity of mutual respect. It was like finding the mother lode that had been hidden in an underground mine for many, many years.

After being in the nursing home for a couple of months he confided that going there had been one of his best decisions. It was the first time ever that he thanked me for anything. As if on a roll he continued and admitted that his trying to convince me to return to Spain had been an error on his part. He realized that I was happier in The United States than I ever would had been in the islands.

With these comments he finally behaved as a father. At last he put aside his own feelings and wishes to place the well being of his son first. When I was growing up he tried very hard to be a good father to his nieces and nephews, who did not have a father in their lives, that he neglected to be a father to his own offspring.

From this moment on we were able to communicate better and enjoy each others' company during the intervals that were my visits. I came to know a gentler father, more understanding, and with an unexpected sense of humor. I am saddened when I think of all the opportunities that we could have had to be close and had lost due to the interference of others.

Our relationship as father and son was brief, but unforgettable. It is the image of my father of the last three years of his life that will remain with me for the rest of mine. I am thankful that the diamond in the rough got polished just in time for me to reflect on its beauty.

In spite of our beginnings I don't accuse my Dad of wrong doings by herreño standards. Today I better understand how it is impossible to live in a swamp and not get muddy. There is a saying that states, "Honor is a gift that the poor man gives to himself". My father fought all of his life against the image with which he was branded and now I see that he couldn't tolerate having a son who would dishonor him. The beatings were painful at the time, but now I feel more sadness than hurt, more anger toward the fabricators of the lies than resentment toward him.

He lived among men and women who were always honing their skill of manipulating others. So it is not surprising that he was one of the best at this art. However, he engineered actions to defend what was his and not out of maliciousness. The following is a classic example of this talent.

After several attempts to prepare his tombstone the way he wanted it he gave up and told me just to do it my way. I responded by saying that my preference would be to keep it simple with few words only. He supposedly agreed. When my father died, I sent an email to a friend as to what I wanted so that he could order it on my behalf.

When he went to check the measurements, he found in the cemetery niche, where the body had been place, a placard glued to a smooth stone with a stand attached. On it was a twenty line poem that he requested be etched on the stone marking his final resting place. He'd managed to coerce people into doing things his way from the very grave!

He did not publish his memoirs while living in fear of the consequences, but he still dared to ask his son to do it. In a posthumous gesture typical of the devious man he was, he left a note addressed to me with these words. "Don't forget to do what your promised!" And I didn't. To you the reader, I present this book; his wish and my promise.

I wouldn't have been able to forget about this book even if I wanted to. It was the man's dying wish which is something sacred to most people. I will not rest until my wife and I finish it because it has cost us many hours, many tears, and many moments of indecision. This manuscript represents the life of "don" Ramón, but also it is his final glorious manipulation.

I remember both my parents with affection, but also with a certain amount of emptiness in my heart for the brevity of the warm relationship. I recognize that among my memories there is a great conflict between the good feeling and the bad, like a pendulum that swings from side to side. The truth is that my father was a great uncle to his nieces and nephews, but he became a good father very late in life. With his death the pendulum stopped, and it stopped on his good side. I feel as if the wheel of the game of life ended up on the slot with the grand prize.

SPECIAL THANKS

Special thanks to my husband of fifty two years for the cherished feelings of comfort, caring, and companionship. We like his parents married for love and started out without much. Together we confronted the obstacles in our path and achieved our dreams.

Enrique and Elizabeth

Thanks to my in-laws, Ramón Barbuzano Morales and Agustina Guadalupe González Quintero, for sharing their son with me. Even though they did not approve of the idea of our marriage, they accepted me and treated me as a true daughter. They overlooked my "eccentricities" as an American, because I made their son happy.

Ramón and Guadalupe

Deep gratitude to my parents, Harold Frederic Powell and Jean McGarvah Powell who loved me with open arms. Since they were both educators, Dad a psychology professor and Mom a special education teacher, they provided me with a myriad of learning experiences growing up: camping as a little girl, living in Europe as a teenager, and financing my college education as an adult. I am who I am in great part due to their caring support in all of my endeavors.

Harold and Jean

www.ingramcontent.com/pod-product-compliance
Lightning Source LLC
LaVergne TN
LVHW021716060526
838200LV00050B/2698